"Yes! An Asian-American Guide to youth ministry! DJ and his crew explore practical and real ways to engage the Asian-American youth. Read these reflections to understand the unique contextualized ministry among the next generation of global citizens."

Dave Gibbons, Lead Pastor

NewSong Church, Irvine, CA

"Youth ministry today in general is an astounding challenge to everyone involved or concerned. Ministering to Asian American youth in this rapidly changing culture and world is even more daunting, since there are so many additional critical concerns that come packaged with over-seas-thinking parents and church adults and their increasingly Ameri-canized children. This is truly a needed resource for the untold beleaguered youth ministry leader/servants out there who otherwise cannot find any help on the shelves of the typical Christian bookstore. And this is an especially unique resource because it is the collective wisdom of obviously seasoned practitioners from this very perspective. Do your church's youth minister or lay leader a HUGE favor and give them a copy of this book. Or at least give them a book allowance so they can buy this book themselves!"

Rev. Dr. Ken Fong

Evergreen LA, Rosemead, CA

Asian American Youth Ministry

edited by
dj chuang

published by
L² Foundation
www.L2Foundation.org

To purchase additional copies of this book, go online to L² Foundation's website at http://www.L2Foundation.org

Table of Contents

Introduction   5

1   Developing Asian American Student Leaders   9
Angela Lee

2   Working With Parents in an Asian American Church   25
Danny Kwon

3   Bridging Relational Gaps   35
Brian Gomes

4   Majoring in the Minor League   43
Justin Young

5   Student Leadership Formation: Goals and Practice   53
Peter Wang

6   A Closer Look: Lighthouse & Wildfire   65
Caleb Lai

7   Living a Full Life When Work is Never Done   73
Joseph Tsang

8   Do We Really Believe the Great Commission?   79
Victor Quon

9   Incarnational Ministry for Asian Youth   97
Brian Hall and Cheryl Seid

10   From Church Pew to Red Light District: Empowering Youth to Fight Social Injustices   110
Eugene S. Kim

11   Postmodern Principles for Asian American Youth Ministries   121
Joey Chen

12   The Humility and Reality of Ministry   137
Joseph Tsang

Postscript   143
Paul & Alice Chou

Bibliography   145

About the Contributors   149

About L² Foundation   153

Introduction

DJ Chuang

Asian Americans are the fastest-growing minority racial group in the United States.[1] The Asian American population is estimated at 13.5 million people, about five percent of the total U.S. population. Twenty-six percent of Asian Americans are under the age of 18.[2] This translates to roughly 3.5 million Asian American youth in America today. They are our future, our responsibility, and our legacy.

L[2] Foundation was launched in 2001 to develop leadership and legacy for Asian Americans by providing support and resources.[3] We are constantly scanning the landscape to identify strategic opportunities where we can be of help. L[2] has observed that there are many great resources for youth ministry available in America, providing generic spiritual encouragement and many transferable principles, but yet something is missing. When we looked for resources that addressed the distinct issues and challenges of ministering to Asian American youth, we found very few. While a number of academic resources exist in research theses or even published in scholarly journals,[4] we could not find currently available resources that captured perspectives from practitioners on the front lines of Asian American youth ministry.

To develop such a resource, L[2] Foundation sponsored a conference specifically for Asian American youthworkers. We announced a call for presenters, inviting Christian leaders experienced in ministering to Asian American youth (middle school & high school students) to share practical insights from their experiences. We asked for presentation proposals that would address one of these priority topics: youth ministry in an intergenerational Asian church, student leadership, and outreach.

We selected ten presentations that were representative of a wide range of perspectives, locations, and contexts. Then we planned an event that we called the Asian American Youthworkers Forum in Dallas, Texas where the selected presenters could share their experiences with other youth workers. We invited youth workers from around the country to this unique gathering focused on empowering Christian leaders and ministries serving Asian American youth. We contacted at least 800 church leaders through our networks and on the Internet, covering a diverse (though not comprehensive) range of Asian Americans all across the United States.

In November 2005, the Asian American Youthworkers Forum convened with a total of forty-two attendees, providing an intimate setting for conversations, learning, and encouragement. Our presenters were largely composed of Chinese, along with two Korean, one Caucasian, and even one Canadian; our Forum attendance had more diversity, with participation from Cambodian, Filipino and Vietnamese perspectives. We recognize that while there are distinct differences between Asian ethnicities, we have much more in common with one another than we have differences. Even though the Forum received overwhelmingly positive feedback, we only scratched the surface of important issues.

During the months that followed, we compiled those presentations from the Forum into this book to serve as a valuable resource for many leaders who are ministering to Asian American youth. We also added two sermon transcripts from insightful talks that were shared at the Forum. What you hold in your hands are the fruits of our labor together, a much needed resource in this field of youth ministry.

One denomination's strategic plan stated the urgent need for Asian American youth ministry aptly:

> Young people will make up an increasingly large percentage of the growing Asian and Pacific Islander population in the United States. Developing specific strategies for second generation ministry is a must. Nurturing youth workers is essential. Developing materials and supporting programs for youth are related needs, because specialized tools and approaches are the most applicable and effective.[5]

This book is a collection of papers from accomplished Asian American youth workers from a variety of contexts with years of experience. Collectively our contributors have served over 100 years of youth ministry! This book is arranged into two sections based on the following topics: youth ministry within an intergenerational church and youth outreach. The two sermon transcripts are placed as "intermission" between sections, loosely based on the Forum's schedule. Since each chapter is independently written, you may selectively read the chapters based on your immediate situation or personal interests. You may use this book for your personal development in youth ministry, whether as paid staff or volunteer, but also as a stimulating guide for your adult volunteers, counselors, and church leaders to study and discuss.

We recognize this book is somewhat limited in scope due to various factors. Nevertheless, this book is a starting point for dialogue and a useful resource. We're grateful for those who joined us on this journey as presenters and attendees at the Youthworkers Forum, and how we all shared many common themes, passions and visions. This seems to indicate what God is stirring among Asian American churches. We look forward to what other Asian American leaders will do to build upon this effort.

On the whole, Asian Americans have achieved tremendous accomplishments with great educational and financial success. But this is not the whole picture. Asian Americans also have significant socioeconomic challenges within our very diverse racial grouping, but to call out the capacity and potential that remain largely latent among us. We hope this book will inspire new efforts to foster ongoing dialogue nationally and to encourage the production of resources. There is much more exciting work to be done.

On a personal note, putting this book together took much more work than I had anticipated. This has been a very valuable adventure in editing and publishing. Now that I've edited my first book, my appreciation for professional editors has escalated.

I'm glad to see how the Forum and this book finally came together with the help of a number of friends and contributors. Thanks to Paul and Alice Chou, Co-founders of L^2 Foundation, for investing in and inspiring a number of us Asian Americans to pull the trigger and do something to the glory of God. I'm particularly thankful for how God provided a virtual friend in the nick of time to help with this endeavor. Special thanks to David Park for providing proofreading and editing help from Atlanta; I hope to meet you in person one day and hang out for hours of enjoyable live conversations.

Thanks to the contributors who've shared what they're learning on the frontlines of youth ministry: Brian Gomes, Danny Kwon, Justin Young, Angela Lee, Peter Wang, Caleb Lai, Victor Quon, Brian Hall, Cheryl Seid, Eugene Kim, Joey Chen, and Joseph Tsang. Thanks to

Andy Crouch and Helen Lee for timely encouragement along the way. Thanks to Abraham Han and Esther Chang for inspiring this project idea from the very start. Thanks to those who provided feedback for this book: Celestine Woo, Christina Lee, Scott Wennermark, and Kenneth Liu.

And, thanks to my own family: my wife Rachelle for this book's cover design and my son Jeremiah for loving life and fun—bringing us laughter for many a days. Thanks to Lulu.com for providing the technology that makes print-on-demand publishing affordable and easy. And thank you for purchasing this book to show your support for this kind of an endeavor.

It would be most meaningful and helpful to us at L² Foundation to hear from you. We invite your honest feedback, questions and dreams, in order to continue this dialogue. We also want to hear from you so that we can together develop a follow-up volume or other ways to serve the next generation of Asian Americans.

Please visit our website at www.L2Foundation.org for current contact information and email us at office@L2Foundation.org with your thoughts and comments.

NOTES

[1] Patrick C McKenry and Sharon J Price, eds., *Families and Change: Coping with Stressful Events and Transitions*, 3rd ed. (Thousand Oaks, CA: Sage Publications, 2005), 325. To clarify this statement, the Asian population had the fastest rate of change between 2000 and 2003, while Hispanics had the fastest numerical growth, according to the Census report, *Race and Hispanic Origin in 2004*, U.S. Census Bureau, http://www.census.gov/population/pop-profile/dynamic/RACEHO.pdf

[2] From *Census' Facts for Features*, April 29 2005, U.S. Census Bureau, http://www.census.gov/Press-Release/www/releases/archives/facts_for_features_special_editions/004522.html

[3] For the sake of easier reference, we use the term "Asian American" rather than the more sophisticated labels of Asian Pacific Islander or Asian North American. To learn more about L² Foundation, refer to page 153 and http://www.L2Foundation.org .

[4] http://www.youthandreligion.org/resources/ref_asian.html and http://www.psr.edu/pana.cfm?m=35

[5] Evangelical Lutheran Church in America's Asian and Pacific Islander Ministry Strategy, http://www.elca.org/cmm/asian/context.html

1

Developing Asian American Student Leaders

Angela Lee

This chapter provides a descriptive understanding of the Asian cultural context, even exploring the challenging question of why many second generation Asian Americans are leaving the Asian church. That alone is very commendable and insightful. The author then presents biblical principles for developing student leaders, and follows it with practical steps for how to do it.

A pressing need of the Asian churches in North America is to reach the growing population of second generation Asian Americans. In an article entitled "Teenagers in the Chinese Church," Youth Pastor Victor Quon expressed concern for the lack of ministry to the second generation even after existing in North America for almost 150 years. He proposed that the solution to the problem of the growing need for leadership in the English-speaking congregations involved making youth ministry a greater priority. He argued that "too often, we look at teenagers as part of the problem," but "it's time to look at them as part of the solution." And he cautioned that, "If we don't do something soon, we're going to lose all of our kids." [1]

One strategy to consider is to develop student leaders in the youth group programs. This would involve our youth as part of the solution, inviting their help to reach their generation. By investing in the development of our youth, both for spiritual maturity and leadership abilities, they will be equipped to contribute to current and future church leadership needs.

REFLECTIONS ON PERSONAL EXPERIENCES

By my senior year in high school, when I first decided to join the youth group as a born-again Christian, all of the older teens in my Chinese church were no longer attending the youth group. Some attended youth groups at other churches; others only attended Sunday services. I felt God's desire for me was to stay committed to the Friday night youth group, even if I was the only one my age. That year, attendance consisted of mostly a group of eighth grade girls and boys, me, and a handful of adults who cared for, taught, and mentored us.

The big age gap between me and the younger teens served as a blessing in disguise. It naturally put me in a place of influence and leadership to the others as a role model and as a "big sister," even though most of the eighth graders had more Bible knowledge. While I could understand why my peers may have found the programs too elementary, I was never bored. Either the material was new and exciting to me, or I was thinking of ways to connect with the younger teens and to challenge them with the relevance of familiar Bible verses. Even without a formal "position" or "title," I had a sense of responsibility and purpose in caring for my younger peers.

During my university years, I served and grew as a student leader in InterVarsity Christian Fellowship (IVCF). I learned a lot about Scripture, leading Bible Study, ministry strategy, depending on God through prayer, and many other things. It was exciting to see what God could do through us, even though we were young in age and limited in experience. Much of what I learned reminded me of what I was exposed to in student leadership training at my high school, with key differences based on biblical principles. The organizational aspects, the principles of peer leadership, and the leading of group discussions were basically the same.

This observation prompted me to apply the same leadership and ministry principles to high school student leaders in church youth groups. I also observed that in many of the positive youth group experiences recounted by fellow IVCF members, student leadership involvement and hands-on ministry experiences were instrumental in developing their stronger lifelong relationships with Jesus. Teens definitely have the potential to serve as student leaders if they are provided with adequate encouragement, training, and mentoring by their youth pastors and other adult leaders in the Asian church. In fact, this potential has long been tapped in most Western church youth groups, and a student leadership model of youth ministry has also worked well when implemented in Asian American youth groups.

WHY THE SECOND GENERATION IS LEAVING

Many Asian churches may be aware that they are not effectively reaching their youth, but might not understand why that is the case. For the most part, ineffective youth ministry is not so much from lack of effort or good intentions, but rather results from lack of awareness or understanding.

Besides wrestling with the questions of "why Christianity?" and "why church?", second generation Asian American Christians are also seriously questioning why they should stay in the Asian churches that their parents attend. Especially for Asian Americans who are more westernized, their experience of Asian churches is often frustrating, irrelevant, dissatisfying, and perhaps stifling.

While many Asian churches may be considered quite successful in their programming for children, the struggle for the majority of Asian churches to remain attractive and relevant to many of their children through the adolescent years remains a big concern. Particularly in middle adolescence, with their growing autonomy (and newly acquired driver licenses), teens may begin to opt out of youth program activities they find boring and irrelevant, and will participate in other competing activities instead. Even for many of the youth that actively participate in the youth program, dropout rates from church involvement are considerable for Asian Americans after they graduate from high school and enter college.

Ling and Cheuk address the common issue in Chinese churches of mixing or confusing Chinese culture with Christian requirements:

> Often the Chinese church in America is preaching Chinese culture in the name of God. It is often done unconsciously, but it is consistently done. There are exhortations to behave in a Chinese way, and not necessarily in a biblical way... Many church leaders have not realized the complexities of the Chinese-American mind, and as a result, do not understand why the youth act the way that they do. Instead of understanding, they sometimes chastise and call for unquestioned obedience. So the questions of the Western-influenced Chinese-American youth may go unnoticed (which is the "proper" way to handle the young people), and therefore, unanswered.[2]

A serious problem arises when the Asian church fails to address the real needs and questions of Asian American youth and instead expects them to act according to the rules of their Asian culture, especially when this contradicts biblical teachings. Failing to address their questions communicates a message that the Asian church (and perhaps God Himself) does not really care about them, or does not have answers to their real questions and needs. Additionally, the top-down approach promoted by Asian culture for parents and other adults in raising teens may communicate to Asian American youth that their thoughts, insights, and gifts are unimportant or unvalued in the Asian church, even though they may be highly praised and sought after in their more westernized school and community leadership opportunities.

Some Asian American youths—especially those who may be more westernized or non-conforming—are frustrated by excessive pressures to conform and perform in order to gain acceptance in the Asian church. They are also often turned off by the Asian church's emphasis on unquestioned obedience, particularly when the focus is on outward behaviors. But wholehearted obedience is both action and attitude:

> It is good for Chinese churches and families to promote obedience and filial piety, since the Scriptures teach obedience and respect for our parents. Misunderstanding from the American-born Chinese develops, however, when Chinese church leaders and religious parents emphasize only the institutionally authorized and culturally acceptable behaviors, or the 'doing.' The Scriptures demand, rather, personal transformation of the attitude, or the 'being' of an individual.[3]

A running theme of these concerns raised by Ling and Cheuk points to an overemphasis on "doing" over "being" as a key issue the Asian church must address in order to more effectively minister to their Asian American youth. Otherwise, the experience that Asian American youth have in the Chinese church will remain superficial and inadequate for reaching their heart issues.

Adolescence may be viewed as a testing ground when their questions and difficulties can be utilized as tools for building greater depth and authenticity in the teens' spirituality, their relationship with God, and in their identity as Christians. It is important for the church and youth workers to recognize the arising issues as opportunities, rather than to ignore or downplay the challenges and questions that are significantly real to the adolescents. Asian churches must provide a safe place for Asian American youth to work through their identity and life issues, both as Asian Americans and as Christians who happen to be

Asian American. The programming and approach to student leadership development should address their needs in appropriate ways, neither demanding too much nor too little of them as they spiritually mature and develop as leaders.

EMPOWERING OUR TEENS

There are many reasons to develop student leaders in the youth ministries of Asian churches. First, involving youth in student leadership communicates that you value and believe in them, and that they can contribute to the life of the church. It is important to communicate support for your teens, and to take tangible steps to develop their potential while they are still young, available and teachable. It is also advantageous to begin training them early on so that they will be more prepared for future responsibilities. Plus, it is always helpful to have extra hands to help out where they can, such as helping out with ministries to younger children or assisting with worship.

As the teens are being empowered as leaders, they are being equipped to become influential members not only in the church, but also in their schools and communities. Having leadership responsibilities makes their experience of church more meaningful, so there is more purpose in learning, and opportunities to immediately put into practice what they learn in Scripture. Enabling the youth with the input and authority to influence how the program is run also addresses the problem of teens finding the programs irrelevant, since they now help determine the quality and content of the programs. Active involvement in ministry also provides a context to build confidence and boldness, as well as humility and love, as they learn to pray through arising challenges to see how God can provide.

As a guideline for developing student leaders, Quon proposes four crucial steps that pastors and lay leaders can take to more effectively minister to their Asian American youth: (1) Teach them How to Love God; (2) Provide Opportunities for Ministry Right Now; (3) Talk to the Parents in Your Church; and (4) Look For the Diamonds in the Rough.[4] He emphasizes the importance of helping the youth to understand that loving God is the most essential part of their faith, and that it alone must be the basis from which they serve in the church or seek to meet their parents' expectations. Youths must be given opportunities to exercise their gifts so they can actively develop their potential as leaders. Pastors and youth leaders can play a critical role in speaking to the youths' parents as well, helping them to see the negative consequences of overemphasizing academic achievement, and to communicate with their children at a more vulnerable level such that their lives provide a role model of trusting God, even in their parenting. Finally, pastors and lay leaders can help develop those "Diamonds in the Rough," understanding that God often chooses to use unlikely people, such as those from broken homes and less fortunate backgrounds; God does not define success in the way the world does.

CONFRONTING CULTURAL BIASES

An important component of developing student leaders in Asian churches involves addressing the ethnic identity issues that the youths face as Asian Americans through not only educating the pastors and lay leaders, but also the youths and their families. For the teens themselves, the Asian church can help them to understand the beauty and strength in being both Asian and American. Paul Tokunaga explains that, "The combination of the two cultures can be a terrific blend. As the creator of cultures, God affirms how he made us." He unpacks this further:

> Our lives in Christ, coupled with our heritage as Asian American Christians, are not without purpose. It is certainly no mistake on His part that we were born into our families and cultures, that we live in America and that we are redeemed. Rather than live in denial of any of these three facts, we should be asking, 'OK, God, you did this for a reason. How can I best bring you honor and glory?' [5]

As they negotiate the process of understanding, accepting, and embracing their God-given identities, the Asian Church can play an important role in helping to empower our youth by fostering vision, confidence, and boldness in place of fear, shame and guilt; thus, helping them to deal with differences and difficulties as opportunities for growth and development.[6]

Asian American youths must also be guided in evaluating the strengths and weaknesses of both sides of their ethnic identity: Asian and American. It can be hard for Asian American youths to sort through and negotiate the two different cultural frameworks in which they are being raised, especially since "Asian and Western values are often polar opposites".[7] Tokunaga explains that while Americans value competition, individualism, independence and technology, Asian cultures value cooperation, community, interdependence and tradition. Much of the mainstream literature providing advice on youth ministry and student leadership development naturally comes from a Western cultural framework.[8] A small but growing number of resources on Asian American church ministries are available.[9] There are four particularly relevant aspects of Asian culture that Asian churches should carefully consider in approaching effective student leadership development for their youth programs.

1. DEMANDS FOR CONFORMITY, PRESSURE TO AVOID SHAME OR FAILURE.

The demands for conformity, with the related pressures to "save face" and avoid shame or failure, provide for stability and a safe, peaceful existence. While it can be good to value fitting in with the collective values of your overall community, and to respect the community's reputation by not doing anything to defame it, placing too much value on this inevitably sets the stage for a monotonous, uncreative, dispassionate, fearful and stifled faith. Such an atmosphere does not foster boldness, confidence, and initiative—characteristics that are important in effective leadership. Additionally, open and honest communication would be discouraged, which in turn hampers the development of genuine faith and friendship within ministry. Conformity naturally rejects the celebration of creativity and downplays the importance of valuing, discovering, and developing diverse gifts among the group's members. An unhealthy and unhelpful fear of taking risks would also be encouraged in the name of avoiding shame or the possibility of failure; thus, it tends to discourage "new leaders" from trying new things. Most natural and/or experienced leaders, however, would be unlikely to commit to such a group setting as they have countless opportunities to serve elsewhere.

2. EMPHASIS ON OBEDIENCE AND FILIAL PIETY.

Although teaching Asian American youth to honor and obey their parents and authority figures are indeed biblical commands (Exodus 20:12; Deuteronomy 5:16; Ephesians 6:1-4; Mark 7:6-13; 1 Peter 2:13-14), the expectations of unquestioning obedience often sets teenagers up to choose the lesser important of the "honor and obey" formula—

meaning they may obey on the outside, but hesitate to honor in their hearts. The traditional Asian model for raising children is a top-down teaching style, where the adults speak while the youth listen without questioning. Furthermore, to maintain their authority, parents and adults often will not share or reveal their problems, struggles or weaknesses. These tendencies create an atmosphere of spiritual pretense where the "parents" or "leaders" are always right, and always must be listened to, even though the fact is everyone is human and fallible. Overemphasizing parental and adult authority downplays the potential of teens to be used by God now. It is not out of God's character to sometimes use younger people to teach older people (e.g., consider Timothy in the two epistles addressed to him).

3. EMPHASIS ON DUTY AND PRESSURE TO PERFORM.

While an emphasis on duty and the pressure to perform helps to promote responsibility and excellence, an overemphasis on these values may promote a "works-salvation" mentality rather than an accurate grasp of "salvation by God's grace." There is also a risk of placing undue emphasis on outward appearances, especially to the neglect of looking deeper at the heart (1 Samuel 16:7). This tends to nurture compartmentalization, so that people separate their "church lives" from their school, work, and family lives. This phenomenon may help explain why some seemingly strong Christian teens who attend all the services and do all the right things—maybe even served as student leaders in the youth group—may suddenly drop out from church and quit living a Christian lifestyle when they leave for college. Also, an overemphasis on duty will result in overlooking teens who don't perform in that particular way. There are individuals who may not naturally "look" the part, but who could be valuable contributing members of the youth group (1 Corinthians 12:12-29, esp. vv. 21-26).

4. EMPHASIS ON ACADEMIC ACHIEVEMENT.

While it is a good thing for youths to want to do well in school, Asian Americans tend to place an unhealthy overemphasis on educational achievement. Consider this description of Chinese students:

> The pressure to achieve educationally and to conform to the 'model minority' stereotype has placed an inordinate amount

of pressure on Chinese students. Those who fall short of superior academic performance sometimes feel guilty that they are personally failing or not living up to parental expectations. This pressure may lead to the use of drugs, mental problems, and/or suicide. Each year, colleges and universities on the West Coast report suicides or attempted suicides by Chinese students. [10]

A related issue is the "glass ceiling" effect which refers to the observation that, although a large proportion of Asian Americans have attained success in academics and professions, they are typically absent in executive, supervisory, and decision-making positions.[11] Min suggests that this disadvantage may be due to the perception of Asian Americans as docile and lacking leadership skills.[12] Thus, Asian Americans will remain at a disadvantage for these leadership positions as long as Asian parents continue to place undue emphasis on academic achievement to the neglect of developing their children's communication and leadership skills.

In working with Asian American youths, it is necessary to help them establish more realistic standards for academic performance, as well as a more balanced view of what it means to succeed in life, especially from God's perspective. Successful intervention with this issue will require working with the parents and addressing how parents communicate their expectations to their teens. In order for Asian American teens to grow in their faith, and to serve in student leadership roles within the youth ministry, a healthier perspective on academics is critical.

KEY BIBLICAL PRINCIPLES

As an important step in defining your approach to developing student leaders, each youth ministry pastor or leader should prayerfully identify its own "set of key verses" to ensure that student leaders will have their beliefs grounded in Scripture. I have identified twelve key Scripture passages that have proved to be particularly relevant to developing student leaders in my Chinese church's English-speaking high school fellowship, Youth Lighthouse. This list summarizes what is emphasized in teaching and training my student leaders, helps to clarify our beliefs, and guides our leadership goals in becoming more like Jesus through relationships and in the programming of our youth ministry. I will outline them here as an example you can follow, modify, or compare with your own. You can also see how they fit our student leadership structure.

The first three Biblical principles deal with basic beliefs:

(1)   EVERYONE who believes in and follows Jesus will be saved, John 3:16-17;

(2)   SCRIPTURE is our guide, 2 Timothy 3:16-17;

(3)   PRAYER is our source, John 16:24.

The next two principles are God's requirements for us:

(4)   The Greatest Commandments, which Jesus used to summarize "all the law and the Prophets," Matthew 22:37-40;

(5)   Jesus' NEW Commandment, that we love one another as He has loved us, John 13:34-35.

The remaining seven principles provide the biblical basis for specific expectations:

(6)   Christian leadership is SERVANT LEADERSHIP, Matthew 20:25-28;

(7)   Being an EXAMPLE is key, 1 Timothy 4:12;

(8)   Dedicating ALL that you do to God, including school, family, friendships, work, etc., Colossians 3:23-24;

(9)   Ministry cannot be used as an excuse to neglect obeying and honoring our parents, Matthew 15: 3-6;

(10) One Body, Many Parts: EVERYone is important to the fellowship for different reasons, Ephesians 4:7-16;

(11) We must be humble, 1 Peter 5:5-6; and

(12) We must care for the poor and the outcast, Matthew 25:40.

Besides introducing these verses through Bible study talks and selecting them as monthly memory verses, we have integrated them through the teaching and training on Christian leadership at our student leadership retreats. "F.A.T." leaders are who we look for among the students we work with: "faithful," "available," and "teachable." Focusing on these characteristics helps to take the emphasis off superficial qualifications. I take the focus off "performance" by stressing that what I'm after is a sincere effort and work ethic versus looking at actual results. Additionally, we place a strong emphasis on the need to care for one another, rather than running perfect programs; in running our regular programs and our larger social events, we challenge ourselves to be patient and understanding with one another, and to reach out to people outside of our friendship circles. I frequently remind the student leaders that Jesus desires for us to be "servant leaders" in the same way that He came to serve rather than to be served, and this is one of the main differences between leadership within versus outside the church.

Without the pressure to perform and create perfect programs, it creates an atmosphere where the teens can try new things, develop their abilities, and practice planning and running different programs and projects. As much as possible, I push for a youth-driven, youth-led and youth-run ministry, where the ideas, issues, and activities come primarily from the teens and are executed by the teens as much as possible. This helps to ensure relevance to the student leaders and their peers, and also provides them hands-on experience in church leadership and ministry.

By empowering students to lead, the role of adults (youth pastor and adult advisers) changes from running the programs for the youth to being focused on "caring, mentoring, supporting and helping" the teens to grow in their faith, to exercise their gifts, and develop their potential. We let the teens do everything they can, while providing them with adequate encouragement, reminders, and assistance in getting tasks accomplished (organizing their time, finding resources, etc.). We also provide adult mentorship and care for both the student leaders and the other youth group members, since they are unable to do this for themselves. We also help them find "balance" and realize this is a difficult process, even for adults. Another important role played by our youth and family pastor and our parent advisers is getting to know, involving, and building up the teens' parents. We try to involve parents (especially of the student leaders) to help with practical aspects, such as helping to provide snacks, setting up decorations for bigger events, giving rides, and serving as mentors when not enough help is found among young adults. This is a good opportunity for the student leaders to serve alongside their parents. We also minister to parents through events like parenting training, so that parents can better understand their teens and can positively contribute to their teens' spiritual development.

Another key guiding principle is to be "kingdom builders" and not just "youth group builders." Thus, the emphasis is not on increasing our numbers, but increasing our impact on the world and the communities in which we live. I seek to build a larger awareness of how the world is a mission field (i.e., their schools and families), to encourage community service involvement (which is typically required for graduation), and to provide opportunities for service projects such as canned food or blanket drives, "30-Hour Famine",[13] and reaching out to the homeless. I've observed that teens who volunteer for student leadership in the church tend to be more spiritually mature, have strong social skills, and outgoing personalities. It can be important for these leaders to invest some of their time in their non-Christian communities by getting involved in student leadership within their schools, attending school functions, or simply spending quality time with their non-Christian friends. To accommodate (and even promote) this need to reach out to the communities God places us in, I emphasize accountability for assigned responsibilities and overall allegiance to Jesus rather than 100% attendance.

PRACTICAL STEPS

Besides establishing your framework of key biblical principles, developing a student leadership team for your youth ministry can be approached as a four-step process:

(1) Determining the Leadership Structure,

(2) Choosing and Recruiting Leaders,

(3) Providing Training and On-going Support for your Leaders

(4) Evaluating the Ministry and Making Adjustments.

Determining the Leadership Structure involves deciding on a structure that would work best in your context. Here are some helpful considerations: (1) your personal leadership style and strengths, (2) your resources within the group, and (3) what seems to work in your particular group and church community. Beyond what you do in teaching, training, and ministering to your leadership team, the example you provide as the main leader of the group is one of your most valuable tools. Because you are ultimately pointing to Jesus Christ as the example we are all to follow, your teens should be able to look to you as an example of how they can offer their own gifts and insights to serve in church ministry. Use your God-given strengths and giftings fully, while gratefully and unapologetically recruiting support from others for your areas of weakness.

In assessing the resources within the group, take the time to get to know your student leaders, counselors, and advisers, finding out their particular skills, talents and interests. You can use application forms and/or surveys to take an inventory of this type of information, but some of the gifts and interests of your teens and volunteers may not have been discovered yet. You can start off simple in your planning and branch off into more specific areas of ministry leadership roles as you get to know your team better. Another factor to consider is the availability of your teen leaders and volunteers, some of whom may be involved in their schools, workplace, and other community activities. Set realistic expectations, clearly communicate them, and this will help them to make commitments that they can keep.

Certain structures may require more or less supervision and help from adult volunteers. In Youth Lighthouse, there was a large group of recruited student leaders when I became the youth director. While the musically-talented students formed the worship team, all of the leaders took turns in pairs serving as emcees to plan out and run the week's Friday evening program (or special event). While this ensured that the programs ran smoothly with minimal adult support, many of the student leaders felt they didn't have a purpose when it wasn't their turn to emcee. My initial attempt was placing student leaders into seven committees for different ministry needs (e.g., set-up/clean-up, communications, welcoming, art, newsletter, etc.). But without adequate supervision (we didn't have a counselor to oversee each committee), some of the committees didn't accomplish their tasks and felt that leaders had failed them and it seemed like a waste of time.

The current structure we have maintains the emcee role, a worship team (which includes a set of worship leaders, back-up vocalists and different musicians who take turns organizing and leading worship), and a team of small group leaders and helpers (responsibilities are spread out by having the small groups take turns throughout the year). Each small group leader is assigned an adult mentor (some adult mentors oversee more than one small group) who assists them with small group times and taking care of their small group members. The rationale behind introducing small groups was based on what seemed to work really well with the youth group's annual Summer Youth Camp.

The Summer Youth Camp is the ministry's big highlight, and the second half of the school year is devoted to planning, preparing for, and promoting it. The camp is primarily organized and planned by the students working on different planning teams, with one or two Camp Chairs who keep track and follow up with each team's progress. Adult volunteers are trained as camp counselors and assigned a small group to mentor throughout the camp. This ensures that each camper is accounted for and will receive individual attention from an adult counselor. Our strategy for developing the youth program is to take what seems to work well at the camp and adapt it to the school year.

Another important consideration in designing your youth leadership structure is to consider what aspects of the overall church leadership structure you can imitate or integrate. Being a student leader in the youth group should mirror adult leadership in the overall church so that it is easier to integrate the student leaders into helping with church-wide events. However, the issue of integration can be more effectively addressed if approached from both ends, namely, to consider changes in the overall church structure. This would involve increased understanding between the two generations of leaders, and possibly creating new opportunities for graduates to get involved in church ministry (i.e., inviting more young adults to be involved in leadership for the main English service, or starting new services for recent graduates).

Choosing and Recruiting Leaders is the next important step. Now that you have your basic structure laid out, you need to go about filling the positions, adjusting the structure as necessary. You will need to decide how many leaders you want to recruit, determining the minimum number of students you want, as well as the maximum number you can accommodate and properly train/mentor. Having fewer leaders makes it easier to invest more deeply in each person, but increases the workload on each leader. Having more leaders spreads out the workload, but it is more challenging to keep track of them and provide adequate care and accountability.

The issue of deciding *whom* you will or will not recruit to join the leadership team can be another complicated issue. This may be dependent on where the overall group is in terms of giftedness as well as spiritual maturity. There are challenges on both sides of the coin—it is important to both not overestimate some teens (such as those who have grown up in the church and/or are leaders within their schools), and also not overlook others (such as quieter individuals or "the diamonds in the rough"). Every teen, no matter how exceptional they may seem, is human and thus in need of mentorship and occasional correction. Every teen is also a person created in the image of God with the potential to grow and be transformed in Christ, and to be used by God.

You will also need to decide on how you will go about recruiting the leaders, whether by personal invitations, application forms, and/or interviews. As you recruit leaders, make assignments to leadership roles and responsibilities according to how the group's leadership needs match with the students' interests and abilities.

Providing Training and Ongoing Support for Leaders so that the student leaders are prepared and empowered to carry out what you have invited them to do. Plan for the training you will provide, how often you meet for training, and requirements for accountability. Also, it is important to provide mentors for your student leaders, whether through your own guidance and/or through the availability of other adults on your staff and volunteer team. Because your student leaders are in a "preparatory stage" for their future adult lives, it is important to provide guidance and support that takes into account all areas of their lives and not ministry only. Help them to maintain balance so that they are not neglecting other areas of their lives (i.e., school, family, friends, preparing for the future, etc.). To care for their spiritual development, address situations where a student leader may be just "going through the motions," instead of serving out of a genuine faith and love relationship with God. Seek to draw out deeper spiritual questions and help direct them to answers. Also, provide accountability and direction for your student leaders in developing their personal devotions, their prayer lives, and their understanding and application of Scriptures.

Evaluating the Ministry and Making Adjustments should be done regularly as you recognize your youths' potential and needs, as your students mature and grow, and as your group inevitably changes over time. Plan regular evaluation meetings to glean input and insight from your student leaders and your adult helpers.

CONCLUSION

There is no single perfect approach or structure that fits every ministry. Take a close look at your church to determine what would work best to meet your ministry's needs according to your resources. You really need to get to know your teens, to discover their gifts and heart passions, and to help develop them. Finding the right approach is a process that takes time, patience, and energy. Ultimately, what we need most is to seek God in prayer, asking and depending on Him for guidance, wisdom, and empowerment as we seek to develop our next generation of church leaders to do the same.

NOTES

[1] Victor Quon, "Teenagers in the Chinese Church," in *Challenger* (Feb-Mar 2001). Also available at http://www.l2foundation.org/news/newsID.29/news_detail.asp

[2] Samuel Ling and Clarence Cheuk, *The "Chinese" Way of Doing Things: Perspectives on America-Born Chinese and the Chinese Church in North America.* (San Gabriel: China Horizon, and Vancouver, B.C.: Horizon Ministries Canada, 1999), 11-12.

[3] Ibid., 51-52.

[4] Quon, "Teenagers in the Chinese Church."

[5] Jeanette Yep, P. Cha, S. Cho VanRiesen, G. Jao, and P. Tokunaga, *Following Jesus Without Dishonoring Your Parents.* (Downers Grove, IL: InterVarsity Press, 1998), 14-15.

[6] Jack O. Balswick and Judith K. Balswick, *The Family: A Christian Perspective on the Contemporary Home*, 2nd ed. (Grand Rapids, MI: Baker Books, 1999).

[7] Yep et al, *Following Jesus*, 13.

[8] A few examples of resources include: Mark DeVries, *Family-Based Youth Ministry.* (Downers Grove, IL: InterVarsity Press, 1994), Ray Johnston, *Developing Student Leaders.* (El Cajon, CA: Youth Specialties, 1992), and Group Magazine (with Website: http://www.groupmag.com).

[9] Sample references have been cited in notes above, by Quon, Ling, and Yep.

[10] M.G. Wong, "Chinese Americans" in *Asian Americans: Contemporary Trends and Issues*, ed. Pyong Gap Min (Thousand Oaks: Sage Publications, 1995), 81.

[11] Ibid.

[12] Pyong Gap Min, introduction to *Asian Americans: Contemporary Trends and Issues.* (Thousand Oaks: Sage Publications, 1995).

[13] World Vision's "30-Hour Famine" is an event to raise awareness and money for hungry children around the world. See http://www.30hourfamine.org/

2

Working With Parents in an Asian American Church

Danny Kwon

I really appreciate Danny's longevity and practical wisdom developed over a decade of youth ministry in a Korean American church. He shares poignant stories as well as the very framework and principles for his youth ministry. This chapter demonstrates that youth ministry can really be ministry to the whole family.

Youth ministry is not easy in an Asian American church. While the work is meaningful and I have experienced a lot of joy in fourteen years of ministering to youth, the work involves much more than I was taught in seminary. It involves more than just spending time with students, more than planning lock-ins and retreats, and even more than seeing the wonderful fruit of spiritual growth in students' lives. All my prior training did not prepare me for youth ministry in an Asian American setting. Moreover, all my years as a practitioner and seminary instructor of youth ministry doesn't lessen certain struggles that arise in the ministry. Let me begin by sharing three stories from my experience.

John was a high school senior who had been part of our student leadership team for two years. Even though his parents were "faithful" church members, they did not like the fact that John's service in youth group took him away from his studies. Before his senior year, John lost his very expensive guitar, worth around $2,000, when someone stole it from the youth group room after praise practice one night.

Mary was a high school junior who was excited to return to Kenya with her youth group after her junior year. She had gone to Kenya the year before. She worked hard to raise funds for her mission trip, trained intensely with her mission team, and prepared diligently. Then one day, five weeks before the trip, her mother told her she could not go. Her mother believed she had become too focused on the mission trip and too unfocused in other areas of her life, in particular, school. She was devastated.

Ryan was a high school junior. He was preparing to go to Mexico with his youth group to serve God on a short-term summer mission trip. When school let out for the summer, the mission team was to meet daily for mission team preparation. One day, his mother called the youth pastor and gave an ultimatum. If Ryan was not allowed to miss two mission training sessions a week for S.A.T. prep class, he would not be allowed to go. Ryan's mother insisted her son be allowed to miss two meetings a week for the S.A.T. prep class, even though every team member was required to attend all meetings.

As youth workers, we all face difficulties and dilemmas. However, the examples above are some of the most difficult ones that I have ever faced. They deal not only with the relationships that I have with students, but also with the relationship that I have with their parents. Hence, as I minister to students, the ministry to their parents must be a priority because they are contingent on each other.

However, this is most difficult because the parents of the youth come from a variety of backgrounds and presuppositions. Working with them becomes a task in attempting to change hearts and minds that are so fixed in patterns of their own desires and thoughts. For example, parents are usually shaped by Confucian thinking (i.e., desire for respect of parents, submission of children, and emphasis on duty), come from an immigrant culture, desire academic and material success for their children, and have certain views of the church and youth ministry. These are some of the foundational ideals that make it challenging for a youth worker to deal with in ministering to the parents and consequently, their teenage children.

Nevertheless, working with Asian American parents is not only necessary, it must be an integral part in order to develop an effective, healthy and vibrant youth ministry. This will have a positive impact on both youth group members and also the families within the church. A youth ministry that seeks to minister to and works with parents can help foster reconciliation between the natural, intergenerational rift between many parents and their teenagers. In addition, the Biblical view is that the family unit must not only be healthy, but also be the arena in which children learn about their faith. In reality, as youth workers, we may see our youth group members perhaps two to four hours a week. However, youth spend more time, at least in physical proximity, with their parents. Hence, equipping and training parents in how to minister to their children will only make our youth ministries more effective.

Finally, effective youth ministry will seek to work with parents because parents can become our biggest allies and aid in working with the youth. For example, if parents believe in your ministry, they will be more prone to sending their teens to it. A little communication with them, even those parents who may be on the fringe, could be the difference to make them less hesitant in sending their teens to the youth programs. Ultimately, working with and gaining support of a number of parents can create "buzz" and support for our ministries. In turn, it can become a greater "evangelistic" or outreach tool than any cool and hip event could generate.

I hope to encourage you by sharing seven practical practices that have been helpful and successful in working with parents in the Asian American church setting. They come from fourteen years of my youth ministry "failures" (and "successes") that have been refined and modified over the years.

THE 7 "C"S OF WORKING WITH ASIAN AMERICAN PARENTS

1. COMMITMENT

Youth workers must be committed to their biblical vision, goals, and values of their youth ministries. They must not only communicate them, but be firm in their commitment to them. Asian American parents may often be driven by different values and goals for their teenagers. They may not agree with what the youth ministry is about or what direction it is going. They may feel that students are taken away from "more important" matters because of the youth group activities and meetings. Someone once said that "a good youth pastor is not popular." Perhaps if we are doing our jobs right in the Asian American church, we will not be popular. We already may be losing the popularity contest, as youth workers are marginalized in many Asian churches. However, we must find our identity in Christ and be faithful to God's vision for our students.

One principle that I have always believed in under this idea of commitment is that as youth workers, we are to be "used but not abused." Youth pastors are used by God, but not abused by parents who want to promote their personal agenda. Often parents who want to work with the youth ministry may want to be helpful. Parents with good intentions may have some ideas, thoughts, or programs that they feel may be "better" for the youth group. It would be wise to listen and pray about the suggestions that parents may have, but we must be careful that we are true to promoting what God has called us to and what God wants for the youth ministry, not abused by parents so that they can get what they may want out of the ministry.

2. CO-LABORERS

Another important principle to remember is that youth ministry starts at home. Biblical ministry to children and youth is first and foremost, the responsibility of the parents. In this respect, we are co-laborers with the parents. We like to use the terminology "walk alongside" the parents. We must make parents aware of their role in shaping their children's spiritual lives. As mentioned earlier, the youth pastor only sees most of the youth group students two to four hours a week. Hence, my senior pastor and church, along with our youth ministry, make sure to promote and advertise that our youth ministry is a ministry that is co-laboring with parents and walking alongside their ministry. However, we do realize that when dealing with parents who are not Christians, we can not initially promote this principle.

Being co-laborers also means that we clearly communicate that our youth ministry is not a place for babysitting and caretaking of children. Rather, we are making sure that the church, parents, and even non-churched parents see that we are a serious entity working to minister to students' hearts, issues, and problems, ultimately leading them to a relationship with Christ that will glorify Him.

The concept of the primary, spiritual responsibility being the role of parents' is foreign to many Asian parents. This was true in our church, and still is for many parents whose children come to the youth group. Hence, as noted earlier, we began by first making sure that our senior pastor and church, along with our youth ministry, continually promoted this vision of parental involvement and spiritual leadership. Tangibly, this means that our senior pastor preaches this vision, along with practical parenting suggestions, from the pulpit. It also means that adult bible studies are continually offered to parents on biblical parenting. Guest preachers who are bi-cultural and bilingual, who can speak to both parents and children regarding the biblical model of family and parenting, are also invited regularly to teach our congregation. We also have so-called "model parents" lead seminars for other parents within the ministry. These "model parents" also continue to provide support with ongoing counseling and aids (which are discussed in the next section). Overall, these are just some examples of what we practice in our ministry to help parents with their role as primary, spiritual guides to their children. Helping parents understand their role as spiritual leaders of their children takes a unified church effort, patience, and a long period of time as we equip parents to fulfill their biblical duties and let them grow into this role.

3. COUNSEL (AND CONFERRING)

Counsel and conferring with parents is a vital part of youth ministry. Parents are offered visitations, conferences, and formal counseling with the youth pastor regarding their teenagers. In addition, seminars, discussion groups, and prayer meetings for parents are an integral part of the youth ministry. In this way, we are helping parents fulfill their biblical responsibility as spiritual leaders.

My church's adult ministries has a cell group model that gives us the opportunity to visit different cell groups to have discussions, seminars, and question and answer time with groups of parents. In addition, our ministry has brought in respected speakers and pastors to speak to both parents and youth about teenagers and "teenager stuff." Some seminars that parents have found especially helpful over the years are "communicating with your teenager," "wise internet usage," and "understanding teens" seminars. Many parents have found these seminars particularly helpful because we are able to explore and unravel the fears, myths, or difficulties that parents have and yet do not know how to begin to deal with them. This is most likely because of the cultural and/or generational gap that exists with their children. Even when it comes to the Internet for example, many Asian parents are still "immigrants" who are not technological savvy. Overall, we try to have seminars that help diffuse parents' misunderstandings and worries, and begin to equip them to be biblically responsible parents.

When it comes to formal counseling for students and their parents, we request that both the parents and student attend counseling sessions together, in addition to any individual sessions that the respective student may have to deal with. To make this a normal part of our youth ministry, the parents are told regularly and consistently that the youth workers are available for meetings with them concerning any issues or concerns they may have.

4. CONNECTION

It is valuable for youth ministries to seek and find common ground with parents so that they can feel comfortable and connected to the ministry. Since many Asian parents are concerned about their children's education, I find it is easy to ask parents to take a group of students to a college campus visit, even if it means an overnight trip to another city that may cost some extra money. Through such trips, we not only have involved the parents with the youth ministry, but we can also build relationships with students and help them grow in their faith.

Mission trips and community service activities are first and foremost to serve God and bring glory to Him. However, parents love the fact that they can also put these "activities" on their teen's college applications. The same is true for a student serving on the Student Leadership Team within our ministry. Surprisingly, many parents are thrilled to send their children on mission trips for the experience, not just to put it on a college application. In fact, quite a few parents have felt a strong connection to these trips and have organized numerous fundraising activities to help defray the cost of these trips, not only for their own children, but to raise funds for the church missions fund and for the missionaries that we are going to visit. I was thrilled to see that a much deeper connection was made between our youth ministry goals and the parents.

Other activities that parents support because they feel a connection to them are: seminars about honoring parents; "applying to college" seminars; career days (Christians with various careers speak from a Christian perspective on their work); and college application night, where students not only do their college applications together, but have prayer and Bible study too.

5. COMMUNICATION

Communicate with parents in a timely and proactive fashion about what is happening in the youth ministry. Sunday bulletins with youth group announcements, bi-monthly letters, yearly activity calendars, and the youth group philosophy of ministry are ways that our youth group communicates. Specifically relating to promoting our youth group philosophy of ministry, we have borrowed some ideas from Rick Warren and Bill Hybels: for instance, we have "Vision Sunday" for parents and students once a year, where parents can come and not only ask questions and make suggestions about our youth group, but also where our first agenda is to present (and remind our veteran parents) our youth ministry's philosophy. In addition, two mailings a year also contain our philosophy of ministry, continually reinforcing and reminding parents of what our youth ministry is about.

First, we communicate our philosophy of ministry to our parents in a vision statement consisting of four parts. Our vision is for young people to: Glorify God (Worship), Gather in God's Name (Fellowship), Grow in God's Grace (Spiritual Growth and Discipleship), and Go for God's Kingdom (Ministry, Mission, Evangelism).

The second aspect of our philosophy of ministry is our core values. These are non-negotiable beliefs and values that our ministry wishes to teach, model, and promote. The core values are: grace-centered, worshipping, accepting, family-oriented, discipling, serving, sharing, authentic, and fun.

The third aspect expresses our model for a relational youth ministry where each student will hopefully nurture healthy, Christian relationships with their youth pastor, parents, peers, and small group leader (an adult leader). Lastly, our philosophy of ministry lists our meetings, programs, and activities which are the means to fulfilling our philosophy of ministry.

The most important aspect in all areas of communicating with parents is that all of these communications are translated into the native language of the parents. It does take more work and time to do this, but it has been an invaluable tool for communication and it shows genuine respect to the parents. In addition, mailings are not only mailed directly to the parents' homes, but they are also sent home with the students to encourage readership.

6. CONTRIBUTION

It is invaluable to get parents involved in the youth ministry with their unique contributions. There are healthy ways to have parents' involvement and there are some unhealthy ways too. Some parents want to be ministry vision-shapers instead of working under the leadership of God's appointed leaders for the youth ministry—that is when it becomes unhealthy. One way we keep things healthy is following a philosophy that we teach our staff, which is called "at arm's length." We want to have our arms open wide for the parents to feel welcome to contribute and help, but not have them so close that they are breathing down our necks and trying to dictate what goes on in the youth ministry.

Another idea originally came from my son's elementary school, and we've modified it for use in our youth ministry. It is called "open doors"—we give parents various opportunities, different open doors, to be involved in the youth group in different ways. Here are some of the open doors we have for parents to contribute:

(1) Ministry Captains: Usually 2 parents who coordinate with Grade Captains when an event or need arises in the youth ministry.

(2) Grade Captains: Usually 1–2 parents per grade (up to 12th grade) who are in charge of contacting the Volunteering and Contributing parents of each grade

(3) Volunteering Parents: Parents who can contribute time at events to make food or support the ministry as chaperones

(4) Contributing Parents: Parents who may not have as much time can contribute by donating food and money (financial contributions) to the youth ministry.

(5) Praying Parents: Parents who commit to pray for the youth ministry.

Having parents contribute to the youth ministry in these ways not only equips them to serve God in useful ways, but also gives the youth worker more freedom and time to concentrate on other matters.

7. COVENANTS

Covenants between parents, the youth ministry, and God provide a very helpful foundation for effective youth ministry. In our youth ministry, we ask each set of parents to make an agreement with the youth ministry, themselves, and God. We call these ministry covenants. We have both formal covenants and informal covenants.

A formal covenant is used for students committing to be on our student leadership team (SLT). Their parents are also required to make a commitment to support their children in prayer, to support the SLT requirements asked of each student, and to uphold the parental responsibility of their child being part of our SLT. This is important to our particular ministry because our student leaders are required to attend a mid-week discipleship meeting. Naturally, this competes with school work during the middle of the week. Therefore, making sure that parents know what is required of their children before they begin to serve on our student leadership team is crucial.

A more informal covenant that the youth ministry and parents make is with the permission forms we use for activities and events. Each form not only outlines what our youth ministry will be doing (event dates, times, and descriptions of the activities), but also the responsibilities of the parents (the times for drop-off and pick-up of their teens). By mutually agreeing to these terms and faithfully fulfilling the requirements, we are building up trust between the parents and youth group. Moreover, parents are taking responsibility for their teens by driving them to events. We feel that these informal covenants are powerful tools to build trust and respect between the parents and the youth ministry—and they've gone a long way towards ministering more effectively to their teens.

CONCLUSION

While working with Asian parents has had its difficult moments, we have found that laying out a foundation for working with parents with our youth group's philosophy of ministry, along with these seven principles, has provided a real anchor for our ministry and for me personally. The statement "A good youth pastor is not popular" was mentioned earlier. I often tell other youth workers and those that I instruct in my seminary classes that I may not be liked by the parents, but I am respected. This is something that is very rewarding to me as a pastor—

being true to what I believe and practicing ministry in a faithful way according to God's word, despite the fact that parents may not always agree. Moreover, God's faithfulness is evident in our ministry as we see both parents and students growing in faith and producing fruit for the kingdom of God.

As for the stories at the beginning of the chapter: I was sure that when John lost that $2,000 guitar that his parents would make him quit the praise team, especially because it was already interfering with his school work and it was his senior year. Despite a little rumbling by his parents to that effect, his parents were clear about his and their expectations (covenant) to the youth praise team, along with the idea that serving on the student leadership team could help him get into college (connection).

As far as Mary's trip to Kenya was concerned, I spoke to her mother (counsel) when Mary was told she would not be allowed to go on the mission trip. I expressed to her mother that I respected the fact that her mother and father are the chief, spiritual guides for their daughter (co-laborers) and that I would respect their decision and counsel Mary to respect and honor it also. Funny thing is, doing it this way, the parents saw our youth ministry's faithfulness to its principles and vision, as well as a daughter who was trying to do things God's way. And Mary's mother changed her mind and let Mary go after all.

Ryan's mother and I butted heads for a few days. I stood my ground and told her that this is the way we have been training short-term missionaries for eleven years at our church under my direction (commitment). I showed her the letter that I had been sending out to parents for over a decade, which showed Ryan's mom that I had not changed our short-term missions program once (communication) in that time. In addition, I showed her a copy of the letter I sent to her a few months earlier outlining the requirements for all short-term missionaries. She soon found a way to compromise with our ministry and respected our ministry methods. She even gave the missions team (contribute) a large donation to spend on our day off in Mexico for food and fun.

This is not the way it always happens in our ministry or in any ministry. Nevertheless, faithfulness to these seven biblically-driven principles along with a biblically-rooted philosophy of ministry has been an anchor to our ministry and it has provided direction and great fruit in ministry to our parents and their children.

3

Bridging Relational Gaps

Brian Gomes

It's been said that ministry is all about people and relationships. Putting that into practice is challenging, and is further heightened in the context of an ethnic Asian church with different generations, cultures, and expectations. This author shares how he's learning to build relationships as a Caucasian pastor serving in the English ministry of a Chinese church.

I have been pastoring in the Chinese community of Portland for the past six years. One of my current responsibilities is to minister to the junior high and high school youth. Crossing the bridges between generations in our churches will always be a challenge. It is my hope and prayer that this chapter will be helpful for bridging relational gaps in youth ministry. The first part will focus on relationship expectations, personal observations, and possible responses. The second part will look at the acronym H.E.A.R. (Humility, Eternal Perspective, Appreciation, and Repetition) as four steps to bridging relational gaps. Although most of my ministry experiences have been positive, I write this chapter with some hesitation because communication and relationships can be fragile as I have some shortcomings as well.

RELATIONAL EXPECTATIONS

There are many labels for generations (Gen X, Gen Y, Baby Boomers, etc.). Each one of these generational groups is representative of a mindset (modern, postmodern, Neanderthal, etc.). These groups also represent a period ranging from just a few years to a decade. So what do these labels have to do with expectations? The labels try to capture the essence of any given generation in a word or two. But these labels project certain expectations of how people of these generations think and act. The problem is that people don't fit into nice, neat packages and don't always respond like their peers.

Regardless, expectations differ from individual to individual, and from generation to generation. The youth worker is confronted with expectations coming from many directions: pastors and church leaders, God, other churches' youth ministries, parents, friends, and students. How does the youth worker respond to all of these expectations?

In learning about the Asian American youth culture in Portland, I realized that I need to see each student as unique and to know what influences they face. Our Asian community is vastly different than that of nearby Seattle, Washington or any other metropolitan area. God is continually helping me shed my over-generalizations and to prayerfully and purposefully learn what expectations each student has.

The students of my particular youth group vary in spiritual up-bringing, language background, cultural influence, and personality style. Depending on the parents, students can have little spiritual influence at home or a lot or anything in between. The culturally Chinese student's expectations are different than that of the student adopting more American culture through the use of language, food, and entertainment. Some students are very familiar with Christian speakers and bands and have very high expectations of youth group. Some students come from homes that mostly interact with two or three other families and choose relationships carefully and slowly. I mentally map these factors on a sliding scale, as follows:

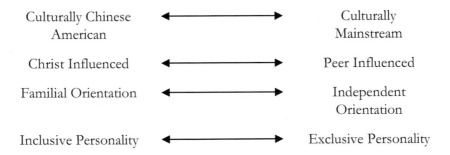

These sliding scales are *a way* to understand my students better. I try to apply these scales to parents and the church leaders also because it helps me know where they are coming from. Most of the problems I have faced in ministry have been from misreading expectations or over-reacting to individual expectations.

I came into the Chinese community having no background in Chinese church culture. My first big mistake was to assume that my previous church experiences in Caucasian churches were sufficient. Seminary never taught me that I had to spend more time building relationships with people before I expressed my plans for the church. I never knew that asking a question that requires a "yes" or "no" answer may go unanswered because the individual being asked could be ashamed since there is no room for an answer in-between. My expectations were far too simplistic. Their expectations of me included having a gentle demeanor and pleasant disposition, communicating in a non-confrontational manner, garnering support from families prior to making significant leadership decisions, and asking open-ended questions.

I occasionally hear about something a student or parent feels should happen in youth group. I am still learning how to respond to this because my western expectation is that an individual will come straight to me as the youth leader. Sometimes, I handle this well and pray about what I have heard. Other times, I do not handle this well and want to have everyone come to me before checking for consensus in the larger community. Even though I am not used to this, I have learned that problems usually arise when I handle things poorly. I have a choice to respond or not, to make it a teachable moment or not, to be humble and admit the idea is good or not.

The same is true when a leader or pastor gives a "suggestion." From my upbringing, a strong suggestion is as good as a command to do something. But I am learning that most Chinese Christian leaders give me the option to respond to the suggestion as I feel the Lord leads. This also means that, for good or bad, I take the consequences alone since it has been implied that the outcome may not be good if I choose not to listen to the suggestion. It's hard to know what to do with implications sometimes. But only God knows the motives of any statement made, so I just need to learn to take suggestions, implications, and expectations less personally and assume the best of intentions from those I minister with. Learn to give people the benefit of the doubt.

For example, a youth worker might observe that parents are putting their youth in many extra-curricular activities that take away from their time to grow in Christ. The same situation from the youth's perspective might be: "Why does my youth leader want me to be at every event? Doesn't he know how busy I am?" And then the parent's perspective: "I am glad the youth leader is able to have so many activities, but I wish he would help my children socialize more." The natural reaction from the youth worker to this situation could be to respond critically for the parents' and youth's lack of spiritual priority; the youth could be frustrated by the youth leader's unrealistic expectations; and the parents might suggest activities that are less demanding. Each party brings differing expectations to this one situation that can result in an increasing relationship gap or it can be an opportunity for understanding and growth.

Our personal expectations of others, our assessment of their expectations, and our responses are very influential in how we minister across cultural and generational gaps. The problem is that just because a response is natural does not mean it will always honor God. Our natural responses tend to be self-serving because we justify our actions to the neglect of the other person's expectations. But if we rely on our natural responses to determine how we relate to people, then we are not honoring them as one of God's creations.

As youth workers, we have two options for dealing with differing expectations. One way is to try our luck with human nature and a shallow understanding of culture and relationship by finding the "right" program, giving a "powerful" message, focusing on a "perfect" passage of Scripture, and waiting our expectations to be met and understood. If we do this, ministry will be a personal rollercoaster ride of spiritual ups and downs. The other way is to H.E.A.R., which is an acronym for Humility, Eternal Perspective, Appreciation, and Repetition.

Dealing with relational gaps needs to be personal. We need to understand "personhood" before building bridges into the lives of students, parents, or leaders of the church. God has made each person unique. Psalm 139:14 says, "I praise you because I am fearfully and wonderfully made, your works are wonderful, I know that full well." We need to keep expanding our understanding and appreciation for how God has made each person. As youth workers, we are in a unique position to positively influence the entire church! 1 Timothy 4:12 says, "Don't let anyone look down on you because you are young, but set an example for the believers in speech, in life, in love, in faith and in purity." God desires for us to learn how to best influence our spiritual communities through Christ-like ministry. That is why I believe we need to H.E.A.R. better to bridge relational gaps.

HUMILITY

The first step God gives us in Scripture to bridge relational gaps is through humility. As youth leaders, humility is seeing the students, parents, and leaders of the church as more important than we are. Philippians 2:3 says: "Do nothing out of selfish ambition *[only my methods will work with me in charge]* or vain conceit *[but I want to be right!]*, but in humility *[how do I respond to each person as you want Lord?]* consider others better *[this is not the time to prove myself]* than yourself." [*Italicized* comments are mine.]

Humility is waiting upon God for the results rather than trying to force them. The apostle Peter knew that even the best of intentions was not necessarily in line with God's will when Jesus said to him, "Get behind me Satan." Peter was trying to defend his Lord, but humility would have been trusting that Jesus, as Lord, knew what He was doing and Peter could do nothing to interfere. Jesus took that moment, and others, to deepen Peter's understanding of humility. God used Peter to pen these words in Scripture: "Humble yourselves, therefore, under God's mighty hand, that he may lift you up in due time." (1 Peter 5:6)

These are some statements that describe humility:

- I can endure the frustration of waiting or the occasional failure because I'm not trying to promote myself, but God.

- I can grow through negative comments because I'm not trying to please myself, but God.

- I can learn how to relate to _____ because God loves them.

- I can change my ministry plans to accommodate _____ because God's plans are more important than my plans.

ETERNAL PERSPECTIVE

As a pastor and youth worker, I have noticed an eternal perspective missing in many church ministries. We tend to focus on the near future in our thinking, planning, and execution of activities. By doing this, we often are not building into our youth an "eternal perspective" of living for Christ. Since Christ is coming back, we ought to make a greater effort to be kind and gentle toward others so that our youth will recognize our attitude to be like Christ. Philippians 4:5 says, "Let your gentleness be evident to all. The Lord is near."

By having an eternal perspective in how we relate to one another, it also shows where our hope is. Our hope is not in having the best youth ministry or the greatest reputation in the community, but our hope is in the LIVING GOD, our salvation! "Love your neighbor as yourself... and do this, understanding the present time. The hour has come for you to wake up from your slumber, because our salvation is nearer than when we first believed." (Romans 13:9c, 11)

What a difference an eternal perspective can make! Imagine the statements below being lived out by youth workers everywhere:

- I can endure plans being frustrated because I'm not trying to promote myself, but God.

- I can grow through personal attacks because I'm not trying to please myself, but God.

- I can learn how to relate to _____ because God loves them and there is no time to waste.

- I can change my ministry plans to accommodate _____ because God's timeline is more important than my timeline.

APPRECIATION

I'm a task-oriented person by nature, so giving appreciation and caring about the other's emotions is not easy. God has shown me over the years how important it is to encourage others by letting them know just how significant they are to God and me. We need to have a genuine appreciation for how God has made others. This comes in the form of showing brotherly love and giving honor when honor is due: "Be devoted to one another in brotherly love. Honor one another above yourselves." (Romans 12:10)

As youth workers, we always need to be learning how to show proper respect to students, parents, and leaders. This means respecting culture, age, position and more: "Show proper respect to everyone: Love the brotherhood of believers, fear God, honor the king." (1 Peter 2:17)

Showing appreciation will vary from youth worker to youth worker depending on personality and familiarity with giving affirmation to others. It is a growing process to learn how to treat others according to God's directives, not our perspectives. We do not determine who deserves admiration, God does.

Some ways to show appreciation for students, parents, and church leaders include:

(1)   Taking students out for bubble tea or lunch.

(2)   Going to school activities.

(3)   Remembering birthdays and special events in their lives.

(4)   Ask parents how you can encourage their children more.

(5)   Affirm all of the positive attributes the parents have instilled in the children publicly and privately.

(6)   Thank leaders for giving you freedom to try new things.

(7)   Thank leaders for giving good advice and suggestions.

REPETITION

The most challenging aspect of being a youth worker is knowing that I need to live what I teach and expect. The apostle Paul challenged the Corinthians to imitate him as he followed Christ: "Be imitators of me, just as I also am of Christ." (1 Corinthians 11:1) Obviously, he expected that they would be mature enough to know not to follow him when he was not following Christ as well. So, the daunting task of living out basic principles of Scripture over and over again is what waits ahead: "Therefore, I will always be ready to remind you of these things, even though you already know them, and have been established in the truth which is present with you." (2 Peter 1:12)

To bridge relational gaps we may have with students, parents, and church leaders, we need to remind each other of God's will for us in how we relate to other people! "Remind the people to be subject to rulers and authorities, to be obedient, to be ready to do whatever is good, to slander no one, to be peaceable and considerate, and to show true humility toward all men." (Titus 3:1-2)

Here are things for repetition in person:

- Be humble by letting God be in control.

- Live with God's eternal perspective in mind—God's plan, not our own plan.

- Show appreciation to people based on their worth in God's eyes, not based on our feelings or opinion of them.

- Repeat these truths and God will give us the ability to do great things for Him.

Here are things for repetition in proclamation:

- Teach your students these truths to help them relate better with others from a pure heart

- Encourage parents by sharing these principles during parent meetings or parent orientations

- Let your pastor(s) and church leaders know how you would like to honor God more in your ministry

- Disciple the youth staff to H.E.A.R.

CONCLUSION

God has created each person uniquely, differently, and wonderfully. Different people require different types of bridges to cross over relational gaps. I've personally found helpful the four steps to bridge relational gaps: Humility, Eternal Perspective, Appreciation, and Repetition.

As you put them into practice, here are some other things to keep in mind. Refrain from making judgments on students, parents, and church leaders and seek to understand through prayer and clarification. Ask God to show you how important each person is. Then affirm those people with those insights ("God has really blessed us with your ability to…"). Begin changing your mindset to wait upon the Lord before reacting to external circumstances. Changing others happens when others see us being changed!

I know ministry can be difficult emotionally, spiritually, and physically. God continues to teach me and change me. As long as we live on earth, we will have room to grow. Part of the relationship dynamic God puts us in as youth workers is to help us be more like Christ.

4

Majoring in the Minor League

Justin Young

Every ministry has challenges specific to its context. As growing numbers of Asian Americans migrate to live in smaller cities, we need ministers who prepare themselves to serve in those contexts. This chapter, written in a fashion like the Apostle Paul's letters to Timothy, provides an encouraging yet realistic picture of what a youth minister can expect in a smaller city context. Likewise, this story will help give insight to the smaller Asian church as well.

A SCENARIO AT A CHURCH NEAR YOU

"The youth group is all yours." Pastor Lin's welcoming words to Jeff on his first day as Riverville Community Church's (RCC) first full-time paid youth pastor were meant to be empowering and encouraging, but they left Jeff feeling wholly inadequate. One month before, Jeff had met with Pastor Lin and listened to the history of fledging attempts to reach out to the burgeoning population of youth in Pastor Lin's church. The first youth group was organized by the parents who rotated leading a Bible study. The youth of the core families came, but they felt awkward being led by adults who were separated from them by age as well as cultural and linguistic differences. The parent leaders themselves were frustrated by these differences, and after a year they sought the help of a younger native English speaker.

They advertised the volunteer position at the local university and a number of American churches in the vicinity, but it was difficult to find volunteers who could consistently commit to the Friday evening time slot of their gatherings. As a result, the parents settled for a rotating schedule whereby a different younger native English speaker would lead each week. Then a year later, due to some leaders graduating from college and others burning out, RCC found themselves with more youth than ever, but again with no leadership.

The church then decided to take the bold step of hiring a full-time youth pastor. RCC is located in Riverville, a small city with far fewer Asians than metropolitan areas like Los Angeles, Chicago, Boston, or Houston. In fact, RCC is the only Asian church in their city and area of the state. Up to this point, RCC focused on reaching Asian immigrants who spoke their Asian mother tongue, and Pastor Lin was the only paid staff. To hire a full-time English-speaking youth pastor would mean that RCC could slowly add to their focus those who spoke English—a move that disturbed many at RCC. But the growing "problem" of youth in the face of well-meaning, but failed attempts in the past left no other choice.

Jeff himself did not grow up in an Asian church, although he did have an interest in Asia and just returned from a one year post-college mission stint in Asia. He heard about RCC from his college alumni newsletter and decided to pursue the opportunity. Jeff now found himself sitting in his new office with unpacked boxes surrounding him. With only a brief and general job description, no manuals to follow, no predecessors to question, and no colleagues to shadow, Jeff was overwhelmed and thought to himself, "Where do I even begin?"

A COMMON STORY AND NEED

As more and more Asians move to smaller cities, stories like the one above are becoming more common. Asian American youth ministry in smaller cities is often pioneering work. Unlike Asian churches in bigger cities, there are no structures in place to guide the newly-minted youth pastor. The leadership of the church, as well as the parents and youth, are looking to the youth pastor for direction and will usually give him (or her) a lot of freedom.

On my first day as the youth director at the Chinese Community Church of Indianapolis (CCCI), my senior pastor shook my hand and said, "We trust you, Justin. Do whatever you like." Looking back, the autonomy they gave a young and inexperienced college graduate at his first job astounds me. Don't misunderstand, I have thoroughly enjoyed the years at CCCI. Despite my numerous mistakes and growing pains (which still continue!), CCCI has been gracious again and again. Although these pioneering ministries have a limited history and a lack of resources, I am convinced that being faithful in these ministries is not only necessary, but will be fruitful and rewarding. My desire is to share my experiences with others like Jeff to make their own transitions smoother; below are some expectations that perhaps will be helpful in this new endeavor.

EXPECT HUNGRY YOUTH

The ministry Jeff is entering is quite young and filled with youth who are spiritually famished as a result of the lack of spiritual leadership at home and at church. RCC's parents are not only first-generation immigrants, but also first-generation Christians. Therefore, spiritual leadership at home is lacking because the parents never grew up in a Christian home, or saw Christian parenting modeled in their own lives. At church, there have certainly been caring and compassionate leaders in recent years, but there has not been consistency. Because the spiritual nourishment has been given in spurts rather than in a steady diet, the youth will most likely be spiritually hungry.

Jeff should respond by feeding them with a compassionate, holistic, and Gospel-focused ministry. This mirrors the example of Christ who, "saw a large crowd [and] had compassion on them, because they were like sheep without a shepherd. So he began teaching them many things" (Mark 6:34). In particular, Jeff should be aware of areas where Asian culture and values have friction with the Gospel. For example, a discussion of grace versus merited performance-based acceptance will certainly be eye-opening to youth who often base their self-worth on their grades.

In addition, despite our cultural shift to postmodernity, modern arguments are alive and well in the youth who have recently arrived from atheistic China. In my own experience, one such youth joined our senior high Bible study and asked the group a straightforward question, "Why do you believe in God?" Further, conversations about creation and evolution are often heard among the youth. Perhaps Jeff should keep his copy of Josh McDowell's classic, *Evidence That Demands a Verdict*, and also add a copy of postmodern author Brian McLaren's *Finding Faith*.

Depending on the youth's age and, consequently, how long they have been in the established youth ministry, Jeff will probably initially encounter different spiritual growth rates. The older youth who have not been grounded may stray before they graduate, but Jeff should trust that seeds planted will sprout in the future. The younger youth will build a foundation for their faith and then grow quickly during these impressionable years. It would not be uncommon for some of these youth to outpace their adult counterparts in some aspects of spiritual maturity. All of this, however, will take time, and Jeff's primary focus should continue to be on faithfully feeding the flock.

EXPECT CHALLENGES FROM PARENTS WHO ARE YOUNG CHRISTIANS

As mentioned above, RCC is primarily made up of first-generation immigrants who are also first-generation Christians. This means that they have been Asian much longer than they have been Christians. Consequently, their worldview is decidedly shaped more by Asian ideals rather than a Christian worldview, therefore, often causing a clash of values.

For example, because academic achievement is seen as a stepping stone to success, most parents will pass this on as the key emphasis to their youth—over and above even spiritual formation. When I started a Thursday night Bible study at CCCI in the summer, it lasted only until school started and then was moved to Friday nights (a non-school night). Even Sundays may be a challenge for church activities as the youth may be involved in math class, language school, or music lessons. Jeff may also find himself battling the great nemesis of the S.A.T. as well. I recently heard about a youth who skipped youth group to study for the S.A.T. After she received a perfect score, other parents decided to pull their youth from youth group to study, citing her as an example. To make matters worse, the parents may not communicate the reasons behind their actions to Jeff given his lack of Asian language skills and their difficulty with English. Then again, when they do communicate with their limited English skills, they may come off as blunt to Jeff.

Beyond programming, attendance, and communication issues, however, Jeff may also find the parental attitude toward his profession awkward. I (embarrassingly) posted the following observation on my blog about one year after starting at CCCI:

> In Chinese culture (at least from what I understand), full-time vocational ministry is seen as a second-rate waste-of-time/mind job. Ministry is for those who couldn't make it in a "professional" field. But I do think that most of the church (including the parents) do appreciate my ministry and don't see

it as a waste of time. So then, how do these two ideas interact? They intersect in this: "As long as it's not my kid going into ministry, that's fine. I don't want my kid to be seen as wasting his time on ministry. He needs to make a lot of money [....]" Yes, these are strong words. I guess I'm just disturbed that while the parents want their children to look up to me on some things, they don't desire their children to follow in my current footsteps [in terms of vocation].

The best response Jeff can give to these challenges is to first realize that youth ministry is family ministry; after earning the respect of the parents, he may be able to slowly challenge the parents to move toward a more Christian worldview. Parents are the most influential people in the lives of their youth (cf. Deuteronomy 6), and a strong youth ministry must partner with them in the difficult task of parenting. To that end, we have honored parents at "Parent Appreciation Nights," added a "Parent Resource" section to our website, keep them informed via a weekly email newsletter, and continually seek to affirm them in the difficult task of parenting. For instance, simply saying, "David is doing really great welcoming people in the youth group, and we're glad he's a part of our community" means a lot to parents. Furthermore, in partnering with parents, there are some parents who are truly looking to the youth pastor for guidance—especially regarding youth culture (e.g. watching certain television programs) and teenage issues (e.g. dating). If Jeff can see parents not as barriers to ministry, but as partners in the ministry, he will do well in staying faithful.

EXPECT MINORITY STATUS

Jeff and the other native English speakers have been and will continue to be the minorities at RCC. Twenty years ago, RCC started as a graduate student Bible study group at the local university. Graduate students were drawn to this Bible study largely because of the linguistic and cultural connection with their homeland. As the group grew and eventually formed a church, the linguistic and cultural attraction continued. Today, people still come to RCC because of the language and culture. In short, RCC is a womb from the world where the members are able to speak in their mother tongue and not be a minority; for a few hours each week, they enjoy majority status at what could be termed "the largest and most tight-knit Asian culture club in Riverville."

As a result of RCC focusing on the needs of native Asians, Jeff may personally feel isolated and lonely because the youth ministry lacks English-speaking co-workers. In addition, the emerging youth ministry may feel neglected from the understandable lack of attention. Indeed it will be difficult for RCC to engage the growing English-speaking population in worship services and other events simply given the logistical challenge of language translation. Further, many on the immigrant side of the RCC may be indifferent to the English-speaking youth ministry. They will certainly appreciate Jeff, but not be involved in his ministry, thinking, "Was not Jeff hired to take care of that? Why involve us? We do not feel we have the expertise of relating to these youth." RCC has historically focused on Asian immigrants and fully incorporating English speakers will be a slow change.

Despite feeling overlooked as a minority within RCC, Jeff should respond by humbly serving the members of RCC and being their advocate just as Christ came "not to be served, but to serve" (Matthew 20:28). During the church's special events, Jeff and the youth group can serve them collectively by enthusiastically helping with babysitting, serving meals, or cleaning up. More personally, he can minister to individuals by remembering special events in their lives. Affirming their success at work, celebrating the achievements of their children, and mourning the pains of their loved ones will be meaningful to them. As Jeff perseveres and faithfully serves the members of RCC, he will slowly earn their respect and realize they can serve Christ together despite language and cultural differences.

EXPECT NOVELTY AND COMMODITY STATUS IN THE LOCAL COMMUNITY

The lack of Asians in Jeff's local community automatically makes his church unique and noticeable to the community. When I tell people where I work, many automatically know our location—despite the plethora of churches around—simply because our church sign is the only one in Chinese! We stand out. But in this age where diversity is hip, that makes us a commodity in a community that is desperately seeking to portray itself as multi-ethnic. The same could be said of RCC. Jeff will probably receive calls for his youth group to participate in the Parks Department's Arbor Day celebration or city's Town Hall dedication—not because they want a Christian witness, but rather because they desire ethnic diversity. Along with this, Jeff can expect to field the occasional phone call asking, "At which restaurant do your people eat? Is it authentic?"

Holistic ministry means he will respond in a Christ-like manner of meeting the community's needs rather than chastising them for confusing a church with Zagat.com. Furthermore, he will use opportunities to invest in the community and be a good witness—not for the sake of Asians, but for Christ! By doing so, he will build relationships in the local community and demonstrate that Christians care about them. As the community sees the light of Christ, perhaps some will be drawn to worship the true and living God (cf. Matthew 5:16). Ironically, Jeff and RCC are in a strategic position to be witnesses for Christ, not only in their own ethnic community, but to the larger local community because of the same reason: the ethnicity of their church. Jeff can be faithful and keep persevering by enjoying these unique opportunities as he ministers at RCC.

EXPECT THE NEED FOR AN ENGLISH ADULT MINISTRY

As RCC grows, the maturing of the younger generation is inevitable: children become youth, and youth become adults. Since RCC made the big step of hiring an English-speaking youth pastor, the church obviously had a growing (and aging!) English-speaking youth population. In five years, these youth will be adults, and RCC will need some sort of English Adult Ministry. This will probably be a difficult step for RCC (as it took many years before they even considered hiring a youth pastor), but an honest look at the demographics reveals the need for an English Adult Ministry. Jeff may currently be able to handle a smaller youth group on his own, but he will need more English speaking adult co-workers as the number of youth increases. But how will he find or keep such co-workers if there is no ministry to them?

In addition, RCC needs to consider starting an English Adult Ministry soon given the close proximity of both the local university and a large chemical plant which employs many Asians. Most of the youth group alumni attend the local university, and hence will be back at RCC during their holidays and summer. Will RCC stop their care for these young adults or continue providing a relevant ministry beyond youth group? The large chemical plant is already the employer for much of RCC's immigrant congregation, but it is increasingly attracting fresh Asian English-speaking college graduates as well. Will RCC be able to reach out to these young adults? If RCC desires to reach out to both the university young adults and career young adults, she will need to start planning now.

At the time of this writing (Fall 2005), CCCI is wrestling with similar issues summarized in the following chart:

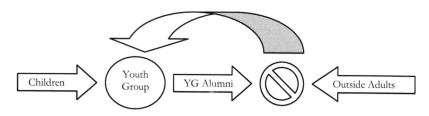

In this chart, an increasing number of families leads to a strong and growing children's program, which feeds into a solid youth program and produces Youth Group Alumni who want to continue their faith journey. Furthermore, there are English-speaking adults coming who did not grow up at CCCI, but still desire to worship in our context. But where do both of these groups fit in our church ministries? As the chart illustrates, they fit nowhere. As a result, they are joining the youth group for worship which is currently morphing our "Youth Service" into more of an "English Service." Such a scenario and its resulting challenges may be typical of other Asian churches in smaller cities. English Adult Ministry is the natural result of both English Youth Ministry and the influx of English-speaking Asians entering the workforce in smaller cities across the United States.

Jeff should respond by catching the vision for English Adult Ministry personally and wrestling with all the quandaries associated with it (e.g. "Is an ethnically Asian but linguistically English congregation proper, or should we be open to even more ethnicities?"). Then he should slowly share this need with the church leadership and members, reminding them of the importance for the church to train future leaders so that God's work may continue. He should also begin to plant this vision with his own youth group, because they are a significant and integral part of the future English Adult Ministry. Such vision catching and casting will encourage Jeff's perseverance by framing the youth ministry in the context of RCC as well as the Kingdom of God.

CONCLUSION

Jeff has an exciting future ahead of him in Riverville. Although his church may never be nationally known or his ministry super-sized, God will use him to minister His saving grace to those who otherwise may have been overlooked. My desire is that others would see the tremendous need and potential to share the Gospel in smaller cities and major in the minor league of Asian American youth ministry.

5

Student Leadership Formation: Goals and Practice

Peter Wang

This chapter provides a detailed outline for student leadership development, anchoring it first on a clear goal, and then giving practical principles. The holistic perspective on spiritual formation for the student leader begins with a good picture of what the student leader should look like. Then the steps for develop student leaders is described based on Jesus Christ's example. You'll also find these principles can be applied for developing adult leaders too.

I have always been embarrassed to be called the "youth pastor"—not that I think it is an ignoble duty, but because of the fact that my student leaders were the real youth pastors who shepherded, counseled, and fed our younger students. Many people ask me, "Is that possible? Do you really expect a 16-year old to lead Bible study, counsel and mentor younger students, lead someone to Christ, and organize fun activities for a group of 100 people?" My answer is yes, yes, yes and yes. Not only have I seen it happen with my own eyes among the students God has entrusted me to shepherd, but there are plenty of biblical characters who were mightily used by God when they were young (King David, for example), and it was only 100 years ago when circuit preachers as young as fifteen-years old evangelized the West. In Ephesians 4:12 (NLT), Apostle Paul urged the church leaders to "equip God's people to do his work and build up the church, until we come to such unity in our faith and knowledge of God's Son that we will be mature and full grown in the Lord, measuring up to the full stature of Christ." It reminds us that our job as overseers is to enable others to become mature, take on responsibilities, and grow themselves.

Thus, student leadership development is not optional, nor impossible. However, many youth workers are frustrated by the seemingly low effectiveness of their efforts to develop student leaders. I believe this is typically the result of fuzzy goal-setting. It is possible to mentor and disciple many mature Christians yet have them all at a loss for direction. Thus, we need to start from the very beginning and examine our basic paradigm assumptions: "What is our goal?"; "How do we measure success?" Without setting the right goal, we will not be able to "lead" people toward it. This is also a particularly relevant question to ask since youth ministry seems to be caught between the wishes of the parents, the senior pastor, and the youth. Ask anyone with experience in youth ministry, and they will tell you that depending on who you ask (parents, immigrant pastors, the youth, or your peer youth workers), you will hear different goals desired by each group. Out of this myriad of goals, many youth ministries fall into ineffectiveness because of conflicts and lack of focus.

After some prayer and searching, I set my goals in youth ministry as the following:

- To encourage students to grow into mature young people with Godly character who can make wise decisions (wisdom)

- To help students become productive contributors to God's kingdom and society (competency)

Furthermore, I set the picture of what a well-developed Christian youth should look like:

Picture of a Holistic Christian

Grace	Orthodoxy	Head
Gratitude	Orthopathos	Heart
Gifts	Orthopraxis	Hand

I believe that we need to help our students reach all three elements in order for them to grow in balance. I often hear parents tell me to teach more Bible knowledge to their kids, with the assumption that "If only my child knows more/better, he/she will become more Godly." However, when we keep on teaching content without conviction (heart) or practice (hand), we are in fact breeding little Pharisees—we are basically teaching our students that we can believe in one thing, and feel and live another. That is why it is so important to have the right doctrine to shape a right attitude, which results in a right lifestyle.

Thus, before we go into detail about student leadership development, we must further develop the picture of what a good Christian should look like, and base our leadership selection upon our criteria.

ORTHODOXY: KNOWLEDGE OF GRACE

There is no salvation if we do not have a personal relationship with Christ. I believe our youth need to learn the following as a foundational part of their Christian walk:

- **Basic Christianity:** Orthodoxy is knowing the right things and doctrines. This is particularly important since the youth are expanding in their freedom and learning to live and make decisions on their own.

- **Christian life:** Christians need to know the difference between law and grace. Although this sounds simple enough, it is really hard to live our life completely based on grace. Christians also need to know the difference between legalism and discipline. While our students may really lack discipline, they need to develop discipline without becoming legalistic.

- **Christianity and culture:** We have to educate our students about the culture we are living in. We should provide appropriate exposure to subjects like comparative religions, the basics of Scripture: its canonicity and its interpretation, Christianity and science, and different denominations.

- **Leadership training content:** Training student leaders requires a working knowledge about servant leadership (Matthew 20) and trainers must meet leadership requirements (1 Samuel 17).

- **Practice spiritual disciplines:** Student leaders need to learn to feed themselves spiritually before they can influence others. Two very helpful books are the student/youth editions of *Celebration of Disciplines* by Richard Foster and *Renovation of the Heart* by Dallas Willard.

ORTHOPATHOS: HEART OF GRATEFULNESS

To balance the increasing knowledge of the student leader, we also must guide our student leader's attitude formation. To help our students develop a grateful heart and Godly attitude, I often ask my potential and active student leaders the following questions—"What are your attitudes/feelings toward…"

- Jesus Christ? (Eph. 2) What is my relationship with Him like?

- Authority? (Romans 13) How do I regard underage drinking? speeding? people in need? (Matt. 9:36)

- What is my attitude toward non-Christian friends? the poor? sinners around you? (Luke 7: 36-50) Comparison and condemnation points us back to the possibility that we still live under the law, not grace.

- Your own sin? (Psalms 51) Am I serious / repentant about my own sin?

- Your accomplishments? (Philippians 3:7-9) How do I feel about my achievements and possessions?

- Pain and suffering? (Heb. 12: 7-11) Am I learning to endure, getting stronger, not complaining?

- Your own talent and resources? (1 Chronicles 29) What do I do with the money from my first paycheck?

Two books I've found particularly helpful for teaching about attitude formation are *Search for Significance* by Robert McGee and *Experiencing God* by Henry Blackaby.

ORTHOPRAXIS: MINISTRY LIFESTYLE AND SPIRITUAL GIFTS

Correct Christian practice is not just to live a life in avoidance of sin, but an abundant life that maximizes God's calling and giftedness in expanding His kingdom. To help students put their faith into practice, these are things that I have done:

- **Teach student leaders how to read and teach Scripture:** Provide training so that they can lead Bible study. By giving them the opportunity to lead, it actually helps them to learn the material. Also, help student leaders to practice personal evangelism through an unthreatening small group like Groups Investigating God (GIG), where non-Christians are welcomed to investigate the Christian faith.

- **Reinforce correct feelings:** Model to your student leaders how to care for other people and not be self-focused. Practical ways to care for small groups include making a phone call, sending an e-mail, or chatting via IM (instant messaging). It may also be possible to develop peer counseling. When we had student leaders who were able counselors, many young seekers started attending our youth group.

- **Encourage Godly behavior:** Help your student leaders be a good example and role model. Many of our student leaders are well-known on their campuses, and they can live out and integrate faith and life. Also, the Bible often talks about caring for the poor and needy, so it must be important. While some conservative Asian immigrant churches might think this is a liberal "social gospel", Asian youth may really think their parents are racist and elitist, that they don't care about the poor. However, since this type of outreach is Biblical, we must obey in good conscience and do so with wise caution.

- **Leading organized activities:** When the youth ministry has activities, youth leaders are asked to help lead them. This exposes them to many opportunities of leadership and encourages them to discover their strengths and passions in areas like:

  (1)   Creative: arts, music, poetry, decoration

  (2)   Organizational: administration, planning

  (3)   Interpersonal: caring, counseling

  (4)   Leadership: vision, motivation, mentoring.

SIX PRINCIPLES FOR STUDENT LEADERSHIP FORMATION

Once you set the right goals and pictures of a student leader, then we can get into the practical leadership development. My student leadership formation principles are derived from the study of Luke chapters 9 and 10: selection, empowerment, inspiration, endurance, training and evaluation.

1. SELECTION

"One day Jesus called together his twelve apostles." (Luke 9:1, NLT) "The Lord now chose seventy-two other disciples." (Luke 10:1)

Jesus "called" the twelve and "chose" the seventy-two. Even though it is not explicitly stated what criteria Jesus used for the selection process, I would suggest these criteria for your leadership selection:

(1)   Committed: I expect my potential student leaders to demonstrate commitment by coming regularly to our Sunday worship service, Christian Education, and Friday night fellowship.

(2)   Relational: I expect my potential student leaders to know how to interact and to be experienced in interacting with people.

(3)   Qualified: I expect my potential student leaders to have a good relationship with family members and a good reputation at school and work.

(4)   Potential: Sometimes I will make an exception to the above criteria if the student demonstrates great potential.

Our student leadership selection starts with a general application process. Anyone in the youth group can apply. However, the pastor and adult youth workers will come up with a consensus of potential leaders and personally invite those on the list to apply. On our application form, we articulate the expectations and responsibilities of student leaders, and expect the students and their parents to sign a commitment form so that there are no misunderstandings. I believe in setting the bar high so the non-committed will naturally walk away, instead of us having to turn them down.

Asians are known for being subtle, not direct. Thus, the process of "selection" is somewhat difficult for many leaders since it might "hurt" some other students' feelings. This is certainly a sensitive, yet important issue. I have made the mistake of creating a leadership training seminar that takes place at the same time that other students were going to Sunday School. The people who were not selected for this special training felt like they were not in the "Advanced Placement" (AP) class and their feelings were hurt. I suggest that it is better to schedule a separate training time for potential leaders. We also found out that the pastor's or youth worker's personal invitation is very powerful. Many youth are going through a phase in their lives where they are insecure about who they are—having a spiritual authority approach them and invite them to the leadership training is a very encouraging and empowering experience. Another suggestion is for the youth pastor and adult leaders learn to say "no" to people who are not ready. It is better to gently reject someone who is not ready in the beginning than having to deal with the consequences later.

2. EMPOWERMENT

"[Jesus] gave them power and authority to cast out demons and to heal all diseases." (Luke 9:1) "I have given you authority over all the power of the enemy, and you can walk among snakes and scorpions and crush them. Nothing will injure you." (Luke 10:19)

Jesus gave real power and authority to the disciples to do the job they were instructed to do—healing, casting out demons and preaching the gospel. Jesus did not want to be the only miracle healer in town. He was not at all fearful of His disciples' development and exercise of their spiritual power. Oftentimes, I observe youth pastors and leaders hesitate to grant real power and authority to their students because they have a Messianic complex—we want to be the only miracle healer in town or we want to be needed (and are fearful that once someone does our job, we will not be needed any longer), but this is not the path of Jesus.

Another reason I see leaders not granting real power and authority to student leaders is because of past failures. They might have delegated to and empowered students before, but because the students failed to meet expectations, the leader then stopped empowering the next generation of leaders. In these cases, I believe it is important to develop proper expectations and learn to forgive our students (what an opportunity for us to demonstrate the theology of grace!).

Another pitfall in empowering our students is "dirty delegation"— this is when we say that we give our students power and authority to do certain things, but we either have not trained or prepared them properly for success. Leaders should not ask people to take on tasks that they are not ready for or are unequipped to do.

By equipping and empowering your students to do ministry (evangelize, lead Bible study, peer counsel, and organize activities), you will build up the students' personal confidence and their corporate ownership of the youth group. You will see them grow in taking on responsibilities and enthusiasm for the activities of the youth group.

For example, our youth student leadership team is responsible for organizing a Harvest Festival for the 300 children in our church. The staff helps our student leadership team draw up the parameters of the program (i.e. we need ten carnival booths, three students giving out prizes, etc.), then we assign different student leaders to come up with booth ideas and find materials on their own. We check back in a week to make sure that their ideas are not outrageous. On the day of Harvest Festival, they are responsible to run the carnival booths; the adult leaders are there just to support them if there are emergencies. We do not micro-manage; we do not rescue them if they fail, but we are there to help them evaluate later.

On the spiritual side, we empower our student leaders to be the first line of response when other students have questions or needs in mentoring, counseling, and spiritual areas. Only when cases are too serious do adult leaders step in to intervene. By having student leaders do the bulk of ministry, not only do the other students in our ministry benefit, but the student leaders themselves learn a great deal as they engage tough questions their small group members might have. Our job mainly is to monitor the student leaders' development and growth in those areas and provide counsel to our student leaders.

3. INSPIRATION

"The harvest is so great, but the workers are so few. Pray to the Lord who is in charge of the harvest, and ask him to send out more workers for his fields." (Luke 10:2)

Jesus motivated people by inspiration, not by obligation. He painted a simple picture of need where his followers were challenged to make a choice in response to a calling for a greater good. In our Asian context, we are often motivated by guilt and shame rather than a visionary call for a greater good. The truth is that our students probably have enough guilt-driven obligations at home, so they don't need that in their spiritual lives. A practical way of doing this is to ask your student leaders the question "Why are you doing this or that (for example, leading musical worship)?" and "How are you feeling about doing this?" Ask questions about how they are motivated. We must also communicate "why" and give reasons for individual activities that go on and how they fit into the bigger picture. As your student leaders mature, involve them in the visioning process. It will increase their ownership and involvement in the activities.

One good method of inspiration is to have your student leaders share testimonies of their successes and failures. Our youth group invited a student leader to share about her experience leading someone to Christ, another leader to share about her experience counseling someone thinking about suicide, and another leader to share his experience mentoring a rebellious junior higher. Having the leaders share their stories can inspire other people to see that they can also do it. Evangelism, mentoring and counseling are not reserved only for professional pastors or adult staff, so we must help students see that they are ready as well.

4. ENDURANCE

"Don't even take along a walking stick," he instructed them, "nor a traveler's bag, nor food, nor money. Not even an extra coat." (Luke 9:3) "Go now, and remember that I am sending you out as lambs among wolves. Don't take along any money, or a traveler's bag, or even an extra pair of sandals." (Luke 10:3-4)

Jesus did not paint a picture of Christian leadership that was easy. Instead, Jesus was up front about the hardships His disciples would face and warned them ahead of time. He prepared his disciples for rejection, difficult physical conditions, and a variety of other complicated situations. The fact that Jesus commanded the disciples not to bring a bag, food, or money was a demand for His disciples' total dependence upon God's provision.

Commitment is required, not optional, in Christian leadership. There can be no endurance if there is no commitment. Certainly, your student leaders' commitment will be tested under pressure (homework, sports, social activities, and many other demands, etc.). But God has grace for those who genuinely want to serve him. Also, prepare your students for rejection and failure. Many of my student leaders get disappointed by the first Bible study after realizing that they have their hands full with 7th grade boys who do not seem to listen to them. This is when I point to our faithful adult volunteer, Howard, who has personally mentored many of these same leaders when they were unruly 7th graders themselves. This becomes a real life example of the virtue of endurance. It is only a matter of time before your student leaders feel inadequate and not ready for the job—this is the time for you to direct them to depend on God and demonstrate grace to them.

5. TRAINING

I have always been fascinated by the passages of Luke 9:4-6 and Luke 10:5-11, where Jesus seems to be so specific in His instruction. I wouldn't be surprised if He had said "Repeat after me..." just to make sure the disciples got it. Yet this is the genius of Jesus' leadership development strategy. In this section, we observe the importance of training, and Jesus seems to include in His training of the disciples, three key areas:

(1)   **Clarification of Job Description:** The disciples' job was to heal the sick, drive out demons, and preach the gospel—clear, concise, and easy to measure. So let's imitate Jesus by not confusing our student leaders by giving them fuzzy job descriptions. That is why we have a clearly written job description for student leadership—so they know what they are signing on for —then design training sessions to equip them for these tasks.

(2)   **Detailed Instructions:** Jesus gave very detailed instructions on places to stay, what to say (the exact phrases); and how to survive (food and travel, etc.). We can do the same basic training for our student leaders as well. There are basic things we can train our student leaders to say and do to help them in ministry; give good, useful, and detailed instructions to our student leaders so they are prepared for most situations. Also, involve your adult volunteer staff to provide some of the training—this will greatly increase their sense of ownership when we rely on their expertise.

(3)   **Worst Case Scenario:** Jesus also prepared the disciples for the worst case scenario—i.e., what they should do when

they are rejected. Jesus helped the disciples to nurture a correct attitude toward failure (in Luke 10:16)—that people are not really rejecting them personally, but are rejecting God's message.

I suggest an off-site, three-day training camp for current and potential leaders. In my opinion, this is better than weekly training, especially for the purpose of team building. We call our training camp the Annual Youth Leadership Summit, and have an open registration for all high school students. We make attendance a pre-requisite for student leadership application. Once they have gone to the Leadership Summit, they can then apply for student leadership. In addition, we screen each applicant through personal interviews. Attendance for the Leadership Summit has increased from 15 students in 2001 to 40 students in 2004. After doing Summits for several years, we have had students who come back again. We started an advanced track by the third year of Leadership Summit. Experienced leaders will ask different kinds of questions and will need a different kind of training from that of a first year leader.

6. EVALUATION

"When the apostles returned, they told Jesus everything they had done. Then he slipped quietly away with them toward the town of Bethsaida." (Luke 9:10) "When the seventy-two disciples returned, they joyfully reported to him, "Lord, even the demons obey us when we use your name!"... But don't rejoice just because evil spirits obey you; rejoice because your names are registered as citizens of heaven." (Luke 10:17,20, NLT)

Once the disciples were finished with their ministry journey, Jesus very intentionally took them away from the daily grind for a time of focused debriefing and evaluation (9:10). This debriefing session included report and observation (10:17), where the disciples talked and shared about what happened. Also included was an evaluation based on job description (10:17) and evaluation based on character development and attitude (10:20).

Evaluation is an integral part of an evolving organization and maturing as disciples. So don't miss out on learning opportunities by not evaluating after every major event such as an evangelistic outreach, mission trip, praise night, or senior send-off. It is also important to evaluate small group strategy / material / organization every three to six months so we can correct potential problems. Finally, plan an annual evaluation party for student leaders that can include the following activities:

- **Affirmation session**: people go around stating something they notice is positive about that leader
- **Self-evaluation and feedback**: Good opportunity for people to reflect on the year
- **Sharing of lessons learned**: Focus on character and attitude transformation

CONCLUSION

There is no greater satisfaction in youth ministry than seeing youth we disciple transform into Godly Christian leaders who exert a positive influence on the next generation. In order to develop your students into the leaders God intends them to be, as youth pastors and leaders, we must first clarify our ministry goal and the picture of a Christian. Once we are oriented in the right direction, we then can apply the six biblical principles of leadership development:

(1)   Selection

(2)   Empowerment

(3)   Inspiration

(4)   Endurance

(5)   Training

(6)   Evaluation

May God bless your efforts to nurture the Christian leaders of tomorrow, as we faithfully and diligently shepherd His sheep.

A Closer Look: Lighthouse & Wildfire

Caleb Lai

The youth ministries of Lighthouse and Wildfire are among the more creative ones I've found, and I hope you'll be inspired by their example. This chapter is similar to a case study in business school, except this is for a church youth ministry. While it is valuable to learn from principles and ideas, it's also helpful to take a closer look at what a youth ministry is doing first, and then examine what worked well and what lessons have been learned.

The goal of this chapter is to bless others through the telling of God's story in Austin Chinese Church's youth ministries, to share the ideas that worked or did not work, and hopefully allow others to learn from the mistakes made throughout our journey. This chapter will also share why we contextualized programs for second generational youth. "Lighthouse" is the name of the high school gathering of ACC created specifically for grades 9 through 12; and "Wildfire" is the corresponding middle school gathering designed for grades 6 through 8. Our hope is that you'll create and develop new ideas beyond what's presented here so that this generation of youth will be houses of light to their communities and that the gospel of Jesus Christ will spread like wildfire.

DEMOGRAPHICS

Austin Chinese Church is an immigrant Chinese church with many different languages and generations within it. These demographics give a small idea of what the Austin Asian community looks like. The attendance breakdown between groups is about 33% Mandarin, 11% Cantonese, 12% English, 21% college, 12% youth, and 11% children. Approximately 80-90% of the families who attend are engineering families; in other words, the father or the mother, or both make a living as engineers. About 90% of the families who attend require at least fifteen minutes to drive to church; some, even more.

TIMELINE

Here is how the ACC youth ministries have developed over time:

I.   Pre-1997

    a. Parents in charge

    b. Saturday night youth fellowship

    c. Sunday school & Joint service with English adults

II.   1997 – 1999

    a. Walton Yuen as first youth pastor

    b. No change to existing program

    c. Attendance: 50-60

III.   1999 – 2001

    a. Gideon Tsang as youth pastor

    b. 2000 – Small groups split by grade and gender

        i. Many college students served as youth counselors, with a 1-to-6 counselor/youth ratio

    c. Spring 2001 – Lighthouse began for all youth

        i. Sunday morning youth worship service

        ii. Breakouts began

        iii. Attendance: 90-100

IV.   2001 – 2004

    a. Sam Lee as youth director

        i. Ministry Teams/Crews added

        ii. Senior Leadership added

    b. 2002 – 2003 – Nita Teng as intern

        i. Spring 2002 – Experimental middle school Sunday service once a month

        ii. Video Game sermon series

    c.   2003 – Current – Caleb Lai as middle school intern

        i.   Fall 2003 – Wildfire (middle school) Sunday service started with different sermon only

        ii.   8th graders given leadership positions

This timeline shows the constant refining and tweaking required of this ministry that we believe to be typical of any ministry starting out. Every year looks different from previous years. Depending on the feedback and evaluation of the programs, many were kept, but many were also discarded. One ACC pastor said that it takes at least two to three years of adjustment (or even more) to have an understanding of where God is leading a ministry.

WHAT WORKED WELL

On Sunday mornings, many intergenerational Asian American churches lump their youth students with their adult English service. There is nothing wrong with this idea, especially if many of their parents are in the same service. For ACC, however, only two or three of the kids have parents who attend this service. The rest of their parents attend either the Mandarin or Cantonese services. The difference between the overseas-born Chinese (OBC) culture and the American-born Chinese (ABC) youth culture is large enough that many youth who attend these adult services feel that Jesus and his message are irrelevant to their lives.

Lighthouse and Wildfire are places where the Word of God and the gospel of Jesus Christ are communicated to the youth in a way in which they can understand and relate (1 Corinthians 9:19-23). For this reason, Sunday morning youth services are meant to give teens and pre-teens a safe way to explore who Jesus is with other students their age. The worship music is led by the youth themselves, guided by a counselor. They are encouraged to find new songs and different ways to worship God. The sermons are presented in words and ways that can be understood by even the youngest of the youth. Past series topics have included apologetics questions, dating, the life of Jesus, "Chasing after God's Heart" (David and his Psalms), books of the Bible, and spiritual themes found in video games (DDR, Super Mario, Monkey Ball), music videos (Linkin Park's "Numb", Simple Plan's "Perfect"), and movies ("Bend it Like Beckham", "Finding Nemo", "Lord of the Rings", "The Matrix").

These youth-centered ministries are developed not only to show how contemporary culture can be seen from a Christian worldview, but also to make relevant and real to a new generation, the practices and beliefs of our faith that have ancient roots. Thus, traditional sacramental rites are brought more into the forefront. Sacraments are beautiful symbols commanded by Jesus that can be used in a powerful way for students to identify with their faith as a global, history-making movement. Teaching the next generation about baptism, testimonies, and communion helps them to appreciate how the church as a body celebrates and remembers its roots. Baptism is a community celebration where youth actually get to see their friends live out their faith. Testimonies allow the entire community to see God's story played out in real and authentic ways. These stories not only bless the students who are telling them, but they bless the friends and family who have come to listen. Communion is a time for students to remember Jesus and his sacrifice on the cross. During the Lord's Supper, we as believers can join with close friends to confess sins and celebrate freedom, take time for individual reflection, and also provide a good opportunity for the unchurched to see a sacred tradition in action.

"Action" is something we have taken to heart at ACC. Students have told me that they do not always want to sit in front of a teacher every time they come to church. They want to take action and get their hands dirty. Allowing them to practice their faith by serving the church and community really develops their leadership and confidence. This age is the perfect time for them to begin to explore their gifts and use them for the advancement of the church.

In order to develop their gifts, we have created something that we call "breakouts." Breakouts are gift-based workshops in which a key component is a leader who has these gifts already and is willing to teach others. These workshops do not continue without such a leader in order to create a healthy environment of mentoring and teaching. Some breakouts that we have tried that work well are: drama/skit, video/multimedia, writing, guitar, along with some breakouts that are based more on reading and studying, like inductive Bible studies and apologetics.

All of these breakouts have outlets where the youth who attend can worship God through their unique talents. Drama teams help illustrate sermon topics and give announcements. Video teams help promote and document larger events like lock-ins and summer camps. Writing breakouts worship God through their words. Sometimes we will have someone go up during worship to share something they have written or we will post it on our website. Guitar breakout students expand their own personal worship to God by learning to play the guitar. Most of the youth who have been in this breakout were new to the guitar, but many of them are now our worship leaders. The teaching breakouts are always there in the event that some of the students do not feel comfortable serving in these groups, or if they just want more teaching in God's Word.

As we worked more and more with the different age groups, we realized that the middle school students were not getting as much out of the message as the older students. Some churches may look down upon this age range and approach these students with the attitude that they will eventually mature and come to understand. This should not be the case though. "Wildfire" was started to counteract that attitude. Middle school students are passionate and loyal. There is still a sense of openness and innocence in them that the Holy Spirit can work through in amazing ways. Wildfire was started as a separate sermon time on Sunday morning to communicate God's word in ways that would ensure that 6th, 7th and 8th graders would feel neither confused nor babied and treated as children. This would be a service that they could call their own, where they would be comfortable speaking out with others their age, and where the seniors of their age range (8th graders) could begin to take on small responsibilities such as working the slides and microphone, giving announcements, and leading games to develop their own styles of leadership.

WHAT DID NOT WORK AS WELL

Some of these ideas that did not work for us may actually work quite well for others. Many of the problems that we encountered with these ideas may have been because of our demographics.

There were a couple of breakouts that were tried, but did not work as well as initially predicted. One of the breakouts that had a very gifted teacher was the art breakout. For students with no previous training and practice, it was difficult to develop and shape this gift from the very beginning. Students may have gotten frustrated because the results were not up to their own expectations. This breakout had very high potential, but might have tried to do too many things at once. A more focused purpose may have been better, such as developing the basics of art. But I believe this breakout has a lot of potential to be something extremely deep and meaningful to the youth in their personal worship.

Another time, computers were brought in and connected to the internet. Macromedia Flash was installed on all computers and taught to students. Similar to the art breakout, this was new territory. The idea was to develop the website into a flash-driven site. Many of the kids were given projects and boundaries to work with, but because of the steep learning curve, the students were discouraged and many of them just used the computers to play games and surf the Internet. Unless well-supervised, the success of this breakout would be low.

For the first couple of semesters, at least one breakout focused on a book that was chosen by a teacher. Finding a good book to go through and discuss is very difficult though. Not all books have a lesson that can be learned in every chapter. Kids also react to books in the same way that they react to homework, except that this breakout homework is not required. Many of them came in on Sunday without having read the assigned chapter because they were busy doing their schoolwork that counted towards a grade. A lot of research and syllabus planning should be used for this breakout if it is to be tried. An interesting book with a lot of new information in each chapter would be needed to make this breakout work well.

A couple of years after starting the small groups, we tried to move our small group meetings into the homes of the youth and their families. Homes are much cozier and laid back than the church because of the family environment. These were popular places to meet and hang out because it was not intimidating at all to ask someone to come over to their house. These gatherings, however, were very difficult to drive to for parents who did not live close by. One recommendation, which we will be trying this coming year, is to assign a home to a geographical area. It would allow for more convenience, but each home would need to be tailored specifically to the people who went (i.e. only a certain age group in a certain area).

LESSONS LEARNED

The majority of Asian American youth rely almost exclusively on their parents to transport them to extracurricular activities. Communication with the parents is essential in bringing kids to the events. If the parents think that the youth event is important, they will bring their children. Youth motivation can and will be trumped by parent motivation. We have quarterly parent meetings to let them know how the ministry is doing. We try to give summaries of how God is working in the lives of the youth and tell the stories that their youth don't always care to tell them. Asian American parents are by far the most valuable and available resource for any youth ministry. They may not connect as well with their child's generation, but they have every reason to invest into the youth ministry. Allow them to show their love in the best way they know how: provision. Let them open their homes to small groups, make dinners, bring snacks, provide car pools, etc. There will be some parents who do understand this generation very well and love to serve God in this way. Find them places to lead in the ministry. Recommend them for deacon positions. They will be incredible assets to the ministry.

Some Asian American idols that we've encountered are education and security. When it comes to education in our Asian American families, the high expectations applied to school are also applied to the church. An overwhelming emphasis is placed on the study and knowledge of the Bible, which is not bad, but there is so much more to the church than just sitting in front of a teacher every time you step into a church. Applying those lessons learned when the Bible is studied is just as important as taking the time to study the word of God.

When it comes to security in our Asian American families, we should definitely be concerned for the physical and spiritual well-being of the youth. However, I feel, as Asian Americans, we have become so completely averse to risk and change that we settle for the same old thing. There is a general resistance to anything unfamiliar and untried. We sit and talk through everything so thoroughly that many opportunities that God brings along just escape our sight. Mission trips are an example of something that challenges both parents and teens to take risks outside of their comfort zone.

High school students in their senior year or entering 12th grade need to be given special attention. These students are leaders whether they know it or not. Because they are the oldest in the youth group, they will naturally be looked up to as role models whether they are good role models or not. Whether in a leadership position or a place to serve, these students need to be involved in building up the community. Otherwise, they may give into thoughts of not being able to fit in and connect with the younger students. There has to be a building up of the community from the top all the way down to the bottom.

CONCLUSION

Work with what you have and do it well. If you have leaders that have different giftings, use them in ways that make them feel comfortable. Not everything has to be done in the way that has worked for ACC. Your demographics could be completely different and therefore certain things will need to be tweaked for your community. You will have different types of leaders and youth. Use what God has given you and be creative. Distinct to our ministry is that we are in a college town with access to a lot of help from college students along with their ideas. They make great discipleship leaders in that they are the closest thing to understanding the middle and high school students, considering they were just there. Their energy and drive match the ones they are teaching. What has also helped in the shaping of Lighthouse and Wildfire was the large amount of financial resources available to us.

The greatest lesson that I have learned in my three years of internship is the importance of my own relationship with God. As scary as it sounds, I can see parallels between my relationship with God and the youths' relationships with God. If I was not praying, listening to God, reading his Word and fasting, then many times I found that my students were not either; the opposite is also true. My responsibilities as a leader go beyond preaching a sermon and handling the administrative tasks. I realized that I am a spiritual leader whether I like it or not and whether the students know it or not.

What is almost certain is that immigrant Asian churches desperately need to effectively communicate the gospel of Jesus to this community of youth. It is not enough for churches to lump these generations together and think that everything will be fine. I am not just talking about creating programs that cater to the youth today; I am talking about speaking the truth of the word of God in the language of the teens. All the other interesting ideas are only secondary. To share the gospel of Jesus in a relevant way requires Asian American church leaders to depart from older ways and to develop fresh new ways of communicating the unchanging truths of God to the culture at hand. I pray that a sense of urgency would be instilled in the Asian American churches leading our generation of youth today.

7

Living a Full Life When Work is Never Done
Joseph Tsang

During the Youthworkers Forum, we heard these words of exhortation for a healthier rhythm of life, of work and rest. This is not only good counsel for those who are Asian American youth ministry or any other kind of ministry, these are words that can speak to the soul of anyone who wants to live a full life.

In between two jobs, I took a break. I called it a sabbatical.

For eleven years, I was the youth director of the Chinese Bible Church of Maryland. In early 2005, I was called by the Vision Church of Overseas Chinese Mission, an Asian American church in New York City, to become their senior pastor. I finished my work in youth ministry in June and started my new ministry in October. But like many youth ministers, I was frazzled and a little burned; not burnt out, which is something totally different, but I was tired.

At the end of the day, if you are tired, it usually means that you worked hard and it is time to rest. If at the end of the day, you are still full of energy and ready to go, maybe you did nothing that day! Maybe you've been slacking off and been lazy! I had worked hard and I was weary but I wasn't burnt out. "Burnt out" is when you can't enjoy anything: your work, your play, eating, hobbies—and for that, you need more than a Sabbath or a sabbatical. You may need a whole life change. But for me, I took three months off. And nobody knew what I was doing. People asked, "So, are you doing anything now?" They didn't know what a sabbatical was. And it is likely that they don't know what a Sabbath is.

The dumbest commandment to break is the one concerning the Sabbath, because I can understand the other ones. I understand the sex one. And I don't always honor my parents—that's really hard sometimes. And what I wouldn't give to have one of those apartments overlooking Central Park. But when the Lord commands us to rest: take a full day off; stop your work; stop your running around; come and enter into rest… we decline, either with words or passive aggressively.

A sabbatical is not doing nothing. A sabbatical is giving my body, mind, and soul refreshment. It's quieting down to hear God. It's learning to let God be God. It's learning to become free to be ourselves. And it's actually living a little, or living a lot.

The Sabbath isn't a prison like we read about in books like "The Little House on the Prairie" or when we envision the Amish doing nothing in strictness—not making a movement, avoiding work of any kind. The Sabbath is for rest; and rest doesn't mean doing nothing either. It's to refresh and to restore. You might even have to work to rest. You might have to exert some energy to plan in order to refresh—like getting some good friends together or gathering the family for a meal. You might have to spend energy to recharge—like playing some football, tennis, or running.

We cannot go 24/7. Our bodies will break down—maybe not today, maybe not right away. Remember the comment we hear about someone: "But he seemed so healthy… what happened?" What happened was a lack of restoration and refreshment.

I took a sabbatical and it freed me. As a pastor, I always had stuff to do. The list was endless and my work was never done. But when I stopped and went on sabbatical, do you know what happened without me? People grew spiritually without me. People still came to know God. Worship services continued to be held. All the things I thought people needed me for… were fine without me. The world goes on without me.

During my sabbatical, I didn't even do anything for Katrina victims. Nothing. When the hurricane hit and left a wave of destruction, I refrained. Don't misunderstand me—I wanted to do something. I wanted to save people. I wanted to save the world! But I had to stop my addiction. My work was done. Sabbatical and Sabbath says: "Enough." It says I don't have to do everything. I can't do everything. I'm done for this week even when my work isn't, because my work never ends.

Taking a sabbatical freed me to know my limitations. Here's what I accidentally learned: I am not God. That sounds absurd to write or to say, but we forget. That's why we try to do everything. But taking a sabbatical reminded me that God is in control and not me. Remembering the Sabbath makes it clear who is God and who is not God. When we don't take one, the line gets blurry.

I was freed to just be myself and I became a healthier pastor. I will not try to do everything. I cannot. I will not try to be the savior. I am not the savior. People already have one. I'm free because I am not essential. I can just do what I can do. I play a role.

I felt like Chris Rock when he was on Jay Leno's Tonight Show. After disappearing for a while, Chris Rock re-emerged and was energized; after taking a sabbatical of his own. Jay asked Chris what he had been doing. Chris declared that he took some time to get off the pipe! He was no longer smoking up. Jay was taken aback and fumbled out, "How's that going?"

Chris responded, "It's great... I can breathe now, I can run, I can jump, and I can play."

He was alive! And that's how I felt after taking a sabbatical.

I rested from my work and refreshed myself physically, spiritually, and emotionally. Our souls don't move as fast as our bodies can. We need time to process. We need time to talk, to write, to think, to complain, to cry, to yell, to run... and to figure out what's going on—which is why so many people opt for therapy.

We need to let the poisons out. When our bodies are tired, they build up lactic acid. If that acid is allowed to stay, it breaks the body down. The only solution is rest. When our souls are tired, we need to release those thoughts, feelings, and emotions. If we do not, our souls break down. I refreshed emotionally by spending time with people. I refreshed spiritually by spending time with God.

During my sabbatical, I also lived. I developed my mind and soul by cultivating my hobbies, believing that my interests were built into me by God. Pastor Rob Bell says that the Sabbath is for living. He says, "the Sabbath is a day to enjoy; the Sabbath is a day to make myself available to myself and the people I love the most; the Sabbath is taking a day to remind myself that I did not make this world and it will continue without my efforts; the Sabbath is a day when I don't have to produce anything and I don't have to feel guilty." That last one especially speaks to me and my Asian culture.

So during my sabbatical, I learned to cook some Southern dishes; I read what I wanted to read, including comics and graphic novels; and I caught a few U2 concerts. On my Sabbaths, I try to get in a good nap and I try to get some good food.

After his battle with the prophets of Baal, Elijah was pretty depressed and even suicidal (1 Kings 19:1-9). The prescription for him was not more Bible or more prayer. It was sleep, then food, then sleep, then more food and then more sleep. Sometimes, the spiritual problem is not spiritual. It is physical. We're exhausted. We need a full stomach and time with our bed or comfy sofa. When I get depressed, I treat myself to a great meal. It usually involves red meat. Then I go home and sleep in late. It's amazing how I feel in the morning.

On my Sabbath, I refresh emotionally by spending time with safe friends in good conversation. There is no counting or comparisons during that time. I'm not interested in who's better or who has the larger attendance. In fact, I'll let you win. Those contests suck the life out of me. I prefer to hear and share stories—to laugh and delight; to confess and to comfort; to share an interest together. The Sabbath is a day for relationship. We work so hard, we forget that life is for relationships. Mother Theresa observed the greatest ailment she had encountered was loneliness. So after that big meal and the big nap, I spend time with friends, church members, and family. It's even better if we can participate in a common hobby or activity!

On my Sabbaths, I refresh spiritually by praying and worshipping, alone and with my church community. I take communion. I read Scripture. I spend time listening to the Lord. The Sabbath is a time to shut down and shut up, to be quiet with the Lord. We rarely have silence in our lives. We have so much activity and technology that we cannot hear God. There's just too much noise.

When God spoke to Elijah, it wasn't in the big and the loud and the obvious, but in the still small voice (1 Kings 19:12). I shut down my work to practice hearing God. I stop speaking. I ask Him for what He wants to say. I listen. I read Scripture. I enter worship. When He speaks, it's rarely a voice for me. I have only heard something audible once. Most of the time, He speaks to our hearts and souls. He leaves an impression or an image. He plants an idea or a picture of what He wants.

Did you ever think about where ideas come from? Do they just spontaneously generate? Do they come from within ourselves? Sometimes they come from other people. But I want to suggest that ideas come from outside of us and some of those ideas come from God. If so, we need to listen more closely.

The Sabbath is for us, Jesus declared (Mark 2:23-27). We are to take one day a week to refresh. Now there are different seasons in life where it's hard to take one full day. There's the season of study, like during finals. There's the season of children, when there seems to be no days of rest; the season of loss and grieving, when our souls are consumed; the season of work, when it demands more of our time. Then there are seasons of extended rest: vacations; down times; in between semesters; sabbatical. During those times, we need to catch up on our refreshment and times with the Lord.

Here's some advice from a famous pastor who has passed on: Mike Yaconelli. At nearly every Youth Specialties conference he ran, he exhorted us: if your relationship with God stinks, don't attend another seminar on hearing God—go spend some time with God! If you're dead tired, don't attend another seminar on rest—go rest! And if your marriage is on the rocks, don't attend another seminar on ministry and marriage—go get a bottle of wine and stay in your hotel the whole weekend.

I would add, if you are frazzled and burned, practice the Sabbath. And if the season of sabbatical comes, take it. And if it doesn't look like it will ever come or won't come soon enough, take it now. It might save your life and more importantly, your soul.

8

Do We Really Believe the Great Commission?

Victor Quon

*God's heart is for all the peoples in the world, not wanting anyone
to perish, but for everyone to come to repentance. God's heart is the
same for all kinds of people in our neighborhood and community
too. This riveting story tells how God can accomplish His work in
us and even in spite of us.*

The following assertion is made with only partial seriousness, but
there is at least 50% of truth to the statement. The unwritten job description for a youth pastor in an Asian church goes something like
this: 1) do all you can to help them achieve a 4.0 GPA; 2) train them to
be well-behaved; and 3) teach them the Bible. If a youth pastor in an
Asian church could meet these three criteria, he/she would be hailed by
church leaders and parents as the most gifted youth worker that God
ever created. But in ten to fifteen years, what would be the fruit of that
ministry? You would have raised young adults who are at the top of
their professions making good money; you would have good citizens
who are models for their communities; you would have a congregation
that knew their Bibles well enough that they could offer detailed weekly
critiques of their pastor's sermons. And that church would be accom-
plishing almost nothing to expand the kingdom of God.

THE NORMAL EVANGELISTIC MISSION IN AN ASIAN CHURCH

The typical Asian church tends to have a youth ministry that is in-
ward-focused. Almost every Asian church starts an English-speaking or
youth ministry because they want to minister to their children growing
up in the church. They are constantly living with the fear that the day
will come when their children no longer want to be a part of their
church. By starting an English-speaking ministry, they believe that it
will curtail the coming exodus.

As for developing a vision to reach unchurched students in their community, the thought rarely comes to mind. If anything, most Asian churches attempt to shield their kids from pagan friends. For example, I remember an incident when a Bible college student did a summer internship ministering to junior highers. Being an evangelistic sort of person, she promptly planned a picnic and asked her students to invite their unchurched friends. During the next week, she was questioned by one of the church elders about the event. After explaining the purpose and her desire to help church kids evangelize their friends, she was bluntly told, "We don't want those kinds of kids in our church."

Is this example a bit extreme? I hope so. Most of us would like to believe that our churches have a genuine desire to bring the gospel to the lost. It is a thought that is long on paper, but short in action. Evangelistic strategy usually comes after the ministry is initially established for children of adult church members. If an English-speaking youth pastor is hired with a vision for outreach, they will likely motivate the church to start evangelistic activities. But then another question arises—who do we evangelize?

There are at least three evangelistic targets for the Asian church. The most obvious one is the children growing up in the church. Adults and pastors fear that someday their second generation will leave the church. In many cases, when children approach the junior high years, their parents begin to panic and demand that the church leadership do something to keep their kids in the church. So a youth or English-speaking pastor is recruited to deal with the impending crisis.

Once a viable second-generation ministry is established, the group leaders begin to encourage the students to start evangelizing their peers. In most cases, there is an unspoken rule that "peers" means other Asians of their ethnic group. This is the second target. It seems like a natural progression since the church was founded to reach unsaved members of a particular Asian people group. If the first generation is reaching out to their unchurched first generation peers, then the second generation would reach out to their unsaved counterparts.

The third target then, would be the friends who are outside of the particular Asian ethnic group of the church, but who are of a similar Asian ethnicity. For example, a Chinese student attending a Chinese church at some point may find it acceptable to bring a Korean friend to his/her youth group. The friend might even be mistaken for being

Chinese, but a certain comfort level could be attained and the Korean student may fit right in alongside of the Chinese students.

There is a fourth target that only a few Asian churches will even talk about. In many cases, it is already on the minds of students, but church leaders consider it a non-issue. This fourth target is the multi-ethnic community. Christian students often have two sets of friends. There are their Asian friends at church and their non-Asian friends at school or in their neighborhood. Sooner or later, it occurs to them that they might want to invite their non-Asian friends to a youth group function. But then they think about how people in the church speak a different language and serve food that would taste funny to their non-Asian friends, and decide against it. The pastors and church leaders might think something like: "Why should we start ministering to non-Asian kids? They already have numerous other churches that they can attend."

Many Asian cultures are ethnocentric. When we think about youth groups, we think about our own kids. When we consider food to serve, we think that ours is the best. When we think about missions, we think about returning to our land of origin. When our focus becomes so narrow, we may very well miss out on things God wants to do through us. He has given many Asians great advantages and opportunities. God is granting favor to Asian believers all over the world. In the Middle East, we are considered to be "safe". In many of the world's mission fields, we can gain access where others are rejected. In America, we find acceptance amongst Black, Hispanic and White congregations. There is a high level of trust extended by other minorities towards Asian church leaders. This has nothing to do with racial superiority. It is a favor that God has granted us at this particular time. It is up to us to seize the moment.

Many students are within an arm's reach of a typical Asian church. George Barna estimates that only 35% of today's teens attend church on any given Sunday.[1] Unless your church exists in some Christian utopian ghetto, there are unchurched teens that your students interact with everyday. We need to spend time and energy in strategizing how we can remodel our churches and youth ministries so that we can reach this fourth target of evangelism.

GOD IS CALLING US TO DO MORE

The term *babysitting* is often used to describe the youth ministry in many Asian churches. It refers to how a youth group is formed as a service to the parents. There is no real vision of training students for ministry or leadership. It merely seeks to do something on a weekly basis to keep the church's teenagers out of trouble. What is the alternative to babysitting? A youth ministry must be designed primarily for the teen. The parents in the church may receive some benefit, but first and foremost a youth ministry should exist for the training and equipping of young men and women to serve the Lord Jesus Christ throughout their lives. If we are merely keeping them from getting bored in church, then we fall short of God's call for a youth ministry.

There have been many well-meaning pastors and adult church leaders who have made this statement, "Our youth ministry is important because it represents the future of our church." It sounds inspiring and intends to empower, but if you listen carefully, the words can be quite deflating. It communicates the idea that teenagers are not important until they become adults. That well-meaning statement says that teenagers are in the minor leagues and adult ministry is where the big-time stuff happens.

Nothing could be further from the truth. In many churches across America, if there is no evangelism going on in the youth group, then there is no evangelism in the church. The tendency of most adult ministries is to preserve traditions as long as possible. We like to hear the same type of speaker, sing our favorite songs, and repeat our annual events. Youth ministries are normally just the opposite. Teens tend to disdain many traditions, wanting their music to be up-to-date and their speakers to be relevant. This may frustrate adult leaders, but it puts youth ministry at the forefront of contemporary culture.

Because of their attraction to activity that is daring, teenagers are naturally more open to doing things like personal evangelism whereas adults find excuses for not sharing their faith. Maybe this is why many major revivals throughout history began with young people. The denomination to which I belong, the Christian and Missionary Alliance can trace its roots back to a group of college students who were compelled to pray for the opportunity to bring the gospel to Africa.[2] Some of them eventually gave their lives to establishing a spiritual beachhead on that continent. Many biblical heroes made their mark as teenagers. Look at the stories of Joseph, Daniel, and Mary and see how old they were, even some of the twelve disciples were probably teenagers when they came under the teaching of Jesus.[3]

Youth ministry should be much more than pizza parties and showing movies. We need to take the opportunity to equip students at this very impressionable stage of their lives. It is one thing to have an outreach event where teens can bring their friends to be introduced to Jesus, but it's another level that a ministry reaches when students are leading other students in making that decision. It's easy for adults to combine efforts to lead a youth ministry, but it's something else to equip students to be leading their peers.

Teenagers are not just the future of the church. They play a vital role in the life of the church today. Because the transitions are happening faster than ever, adults will not be able to keep up on their own. They are going to be the ones that will guide adults through the changes that are coming to our society. We need spiritually anointed young men and women to demonstrate for us how the church can express the gospel message in a way that remains fresh and relevant. But unknowingly, many of our churches today are putting a severe handicap on our youth ministries. We teach them about the Great Commission and how Christ has called us to reach the world, but if we do an outreach program, we limit them to reaching out only to other Asians. As a reflection of the total population of the United States, we could refer to this as the 4.2% Great Commission.[4]

Some adult youth leaders might object to this statement by saying, "We welcome any youth, no matter what ethnic group they represent, to be a part of our ministry." The point here is not just what you say, but how do you really make that happen? Can a Caucasian kid be on your worship team? Will an African American teen have the opportunity to be a leader? Can you see a Hispanic student leading one of your Bible studies?

Some church leaders might want to re-examine the Great Commission passages. They will point to Acts 1:8—"... and you will be my witnesses in Jerusalem, and in all Judea and Samaria, and to the ends of the earth." They will point out how we have to reach the kids in our Jerusalem first, and then proceed to Judea and Samaria before we finally reach the ends of the earth. The problem with this is that most scholars believe that the Great Commission targets Jerusalem, Judea and Samaria and the ends of the earth simultaneously, not sequentially. We do missions (the ends of the earth) while we also reach people in

Jerusalem (other Asians) and Judea and Samaria (other ethnic kids within our reach).

Naturally, not every church is called to reach every people group, but our youth ministries should be a reflection of the student population in our neighborhoods or in the schools that our students attend. This means that if one of our church kids meets another student in the normal walk of life, then that other student should be considered someone within reasonable reach of our church's teenagers.

The focus of most Asian youth ministries is to keep the church kids in the church. Our biggest fear is to have our church fall victim to that mythical 80% statistic—that 80% of our kids will eventually leave the church. No one has ever verified this figure with research. It is what we are observing in our own ministries, but these young men and women are not leaving the faith, only the immigrant church. The most significant transition that has to happen in Asian churches is the move from building our church to building the kingdom. The Great Commission never instructs us to bring everyone into our church; the instructions are to go and to make disciples. This doesn't happen by keeping everyone in the same place. Once we turn our focus inward, we are inviting a slow death to our ministry.

If we really believe the Great Commission, we need to turn our focus toward kingdom-minded activity. We cannot create Asian ghettos for our students and expect the world to come to us. To be kingdom-minded means shaping your youth group into something designed for students outside of your church. In the process of creating a youth ministry for someone else, you'll surprisingly have a church that your own students will love to call their spiritual home.

This is the story of how God did this for us at the San Jose Chinese Alliance Church. You will see how true some of the principles discussed above came true in our ministry. The irony in the story is that we did not plan this at the outset. We were not intentional. The Holy Spirit led us every step of the way.

WHAT HAPPENED AT THE SAN JOSE CHINESE ALLIANCE CHURCH, 1997-2002

The youth ministry at the San Jose Chinese Alliance Church (SJCAC) had experienced fairly regular growth in the early 1990's. But in 1996, we hit a plateau when numbers remained constant. Of greater concern was the fact that our students were getting too cozy with one another. They liked coming to youth events and really enjoyed each other's company. This was good for fellowship, but stagnating for evangelism. There was only an obligatory concern for spiritually lost friends.

After doing some research in Santa Clara County, it became clear to me that even with some fairly large youth groups in the area, that we were only reaching a fraction of the unchurched students in the area. Receiving inspiration from our denomination's practice of planting new churches, I determined that we were going to plant a new youth group. I knew that youth groups, like churches, all reach a saturation point. Our high school group of fifty students and junior high group of thirty would probably never grow significantly past those numbers. If we were going to reach other teens with the gospel, we would have to start a new group.

Since most of our kids came from the west side of Silicon Valley, I figured that would be the best place to start. It seemed logical in light of the fact that the region had the highest concentration of Asian families and where we had the most personal contacts; funny how God likes to blow logic out of the water.

The first step was to share this idea with our student ministry team. I knew that there would be some resistance, but they would have to be the ones to reach other students, so it was vital to get their support. As expected, my student leaders were aghast. They had visions of being split up into regional youth groups. They panicked and had thoughts of never seeing each other again. I calmed them down and reassured them that nobody was going to force anything on them. Those who would want to start a new youth group would have to pray and be called by God to do it. By the next month's meeting, if there were no volunteers, then we would not do it.

My second move was to share the idea with our youth congregation. We have a Sunday morning youth service every week and I chose a particular Sunday to preach on the subject. I asked if there were any students willing to help with this project to come and see me after the service. I didn't expect anyone to come forward, but after the closing prayer, one student came forward. His name was Jason Ma. This really surprised me because Jason was the last person I expected since he was not a regular attendee, came from a broken home, and went through a variety of teenage rebellion episodes. Little did I know that God had

been working in Jason's life and he was in the midst of a personal revival. He offered to help, but I didn't think that it would amount to
much. God had to work on me.

In the meantime, I met with our ministry team again, not quite sure
what to expect. To my surprise, three of the student leaders said that
they had been praying about this opportunity and believed that God
was leading them to participate. I was ecstatic and began to quickly lay
out plans to reach unchurched Asian students on the west side of Silicon Valley. The three students quickly stopped me and shared that they
believed that God wanted us to reach the east side (where the church
building is located). Their reasoning was that our youth ministry was
already in touch with many students on the west side. The area we had
not reached was the east side. All three of them lived in that section of
town. I hesitated momentarily, and realized they were right.

We planned for a new ministry team to start this new youth group.
During that same year, the Billy Graham Crusade was coming to the
San Francisco Bay Area. One of the nights was designated as youth
night and our church had prepared to participate. On the day before
the crusade, Jason called and asked me to save twenty seats for him
because he was bringing some friends that night. Again, I had my
doubts. Why would Jason come to the crusade and why would twenty
of his friends want to join him? It didn't make sense. Sure enough, Jason came and brought his twenty friends. Some of them even walked
down to receive Christ. When the counselor asked them, "What church
did you come with?", the guys only gave him blank stares. They didn't
come with a church, they came with Jason.

I finally began to see that God was doing something quite extraor-
dinary. Jason joined the ministry team along with four others. What was
missing were adult volunteers. Then one day after Sunday service, I ran
into Clara Chau, one of my former students, who had just happened to
return to the Bay Area. As I shared with her about the new youth
group, Clara's face broke into a big smile. She had been sensing that
God was leading her to some kind of urban outreach and this new
youth group was quite intriguing. She soon became part of the
team and was joined by two other adventurous adults, Lan Hoang and
Mark Tran.

The team began meeting in the fall and was anxious to start the
new group. They wanted to start right away, but I encouraged them to
pray and meet together a little longer. We decided upon the name

S.O.U.L., an acronym for Shine On Us, Lord. We started the group on Tuesday night, February 3rd, 1998. We weren't sure what to expect. Twelve of us from the church came to the first meeting. Eventually, we were joined by seventeen others, most of whom had never set foot inside a church before.

At first, I questioned why the students wanted to meet on Tuesdays. After all, the church had its prayer meetings on Wednesday. Why not meet on the same night and spare us from having to open the doors on another night? But after seeing the students who were coming to S.O.U.L. and envisioning the frightened look that would come upon church members' faces, I quickly deduced that Tuesday was indeed a great night for S.O.U.L. meetings to take place.

S.O.U.L. began to grow. Students from all over the east side began to check it out. The most amazing thing was that most of them were not Chinese. We had African Americans, Hispanics, Filipinos, Cambodians, Vietnamese, Persians and even some Caucasian students. All of them were either unchurched or had rejected the traditional church background that they had while growing up. We soon figured out that this was not like the other youth groups in the church. We had a sense that the Holy Spirit was writing out the ministry plan for us on a week-to-week basis. Jason began to do a lot of the speaking. Many of those who came were either his friends or had known him. They trusted him. Clara had to work with Jason a little bit, because his language was not entirely holy yet, but there was no mistaking that Jason was different and that God was transforming his life.

Over the next two years, we had some interesting experiences with S.O.U.L. Breakdancing was a favorite activity. Young men would come to our church to practice their moves because they knew it was a safe place to dance. Nobody would hassle them or hit on them for drugs. Cigarette butts were also a common occurrence. Somehow they knew that the church was not a place to smoke. So prior to entering the building, they would dispose of their cigarettes. It left a little bit of a mess in the entryways, but it was obvious that they respected God's house.

Worship was difficult to incorporate because the kids didn't know the Christian songs. But when the program was finished, many of them would grab the drums and guitars and start playing the music that they knew. Many were listening to Jason's and Clara's messages. Some of them came to our youth camps. It wasn't long before some of them accepted Christ. We began to hear some of their stories. It seemed like every Tuesday night, someone either had prayed to receive Christ, was delivered from some demonic force, or had received a unique and personal experience of God.

Of course, not everything went smoothly. Once word got around that something called S.O.U.L. was happening on Tuesday nights, parents of our regular youth and church leaders became concerned. Parents began e-mailing each other and we had quite a controversy on our hands. One of the e-mails expressed some of the parents' deep concerns about the strange hair colors and jewelry that some of the S.O.U.L. kids would wear. They feared these street kids might use slang and profanity at church. Their biggest concern was how the S.O.U.L. couples would hold hands and show public affection for each other. The final words were, "We don't want our church kids to be like the S.O.U.L. kids." They believed that it was the job of the youth ministry to shelter their own kids from the evil influences of the world. The parents felt like they had to spend all week protecting their children from bad kids at school. They thought, "At least we don't have to worry about them at church." Now with S.O.U.L., would the church be able to handle kids with all these social and behavioral problems? The issue finally came to a church board meeting where God did a significant thing.

After hearing the concerns of some of the board members, the church's senior pastor, Abraham Poon, spoke out in favor of S.O.U.L. He said that when the church had purchased the property upon which our buildings sat, one of statements made was a desire to bring the gospel to the people in the neighborhood where the land was located. He believed that S.O.U.L. was the beginning of the fulfillment of that vision. Later on, he encouraged board members to lead their congregations to engage the S.O.U.L. kids in ministry. Pastor Poon's courageous endorsement paved the way for S.O.U.L. to develop and flourish as a multicultural ministry in a Chinese immigrant church.

Around the same time, one of the church parents responded to the barrage of concerned e-mails. Gus was not only a church parent, he was also a volunteer youth Sunday School teacher. He had attended the most recent youth winter retreat which included a number of students from S.O.U.L. Gus told the other parents of his initial reaction to the kids. He was shocked. He had never seen kids like this at a church event. He wondered why they were at the retreat and how we were going to keep an eye on them for the entire weekend. Gus was uneasy with the behavior of these kids during the retreat program. They were loud and difficult to control, but then he noticed that they were quite interested in the Bible studies and intent on listening to our speaker. Gus began to notice an interest and hunger for spiritual things (something he had not always seen in church kids). On the final night, when many of the S.O.U.L. kids made professions of faith and confessions of sin, Gus realized he was seeing genuine life transformation happening right in front of him and convinced him that S.O.U.L. was exactly the kind of ministry that our church needed to be involved in. When he testified of the change that had occurred in his heart, it strongly influenced the opinions of many of the other parents in the church.

While there was still a desire in some of the parents for their kids not to become like the S.O.U.L. kids, God took care of this as well. One night, some of the guys showed up early for S.O.U.L. They were hanging around the church basketball court when they noticed a car pulling up on the street next to the church fence. They saw a couple in the car with the man yelling at the woman. And then he started to hit her. Two S.O.U.L. guys ran and jumped the fence and came to the woman's rescue. As it turned out, the woman was pregnant and the man wanted her to abort the baby or else he would throw her out of his apartment. The woman had refused. The two S.O.U.L. guys went back to the apartment and helped the woman collect her things and made sure that she could leave safely. After assisting her, they brought her back to the S.O.U.L. meeting and told the leaders what had happened. People gathered around to pray for the woman while one of her rescuers called his mother. It just so happened that his mom worked in a shelter for battered women. They were able to get her a place to stay until she could be reunited with her family. When I heard this story, I wrote about it in our church newsletter. I concluded the story with the statement, "I hope that more of our church kids can learn to be like the guys in S.O.U.L."

What do you do with kids who receive Christ? You disciple them, of course. With S.O.U.L., that was easier said than done. They were not as academic as our church kids and did not respond very enthusiastically to the normal methods of discipleship. One thing we soon discovered was that S.O.U.L. was going to be something entirely different from anything our youth ministry had ever done. We wrote our own discipleship manual for S.O.U.L. and it was not a nice, neat package of

Christian topics. We began to focus on life experiences. The discipleship was based on how God helps us to handle times of anger, sadness, triumph, and discovering God's plan for our lives. We didn't do discipleship inside a church classroom. We recalled that Jesus discipled his followers on the street as they experienced life together and we decided to do the same thing. Our leaders took kids to the mall, the police station, and even to a cemetery. The results were much more encouraging with the SOUL Discipleship manual. Some kids decided to be baptized and to become church members.

WHAT WAS OUR PLAN?

If I can be quite honest about the whole S.O.U.L. phenomenon, my volunteer leaders and I had no plans for such a ministry. There was no strategy for reaching students from different ethnic backgrounds. I wish I could tell everyone today that we had this great love for non-Chinese students in our neighborhoods and that we were moved by the power of God to reach them, but that wouldn't be honest. We had no such plan.

We did have another sort of plan. It was much broader than just reaching multiethnic students. We refused to accept the idea that the purpose of youth ministry was to evangelize and protect those already in the church. We knew that the heart of God is for those who are spiritually lost. Limiting our youth ministry to eighty students and our outreach focus to 4.2% of the population was not acceptable to us. S.O.U.L. was birthed in the prayers of our leaders to seek ways to empower our students to reach a wider scope of friends with the gospel.

Our original plan was not to start a multiethnic youth ministry, it was to take the Great Commission seriously. After sharing this idea with adult volunteers and then with student leaders, we began to pray together. Once we started seeking God for a strategy to expand our territory, he began to unravel the mystery for us. He gave me the idea of planting a new youth group; he provided Jason Ma as a student leader to gather unchurched youth; and he gave revelation to Pastor Poon to give much needed approval. All three of us played vital roles in the establishment of S.O.U.L. God began to speak to students to join the effort to get the new youth group off the ground, all the while taking time to carefully pray through a strategy; and in time, God's plan was revealed to us.

One of the unexpected side benefits of starting S.O.U.L. was that it also showed us how to more effectively reach church kids and their friends. Once we knew that the Holy Spirit was leading us to reach out to multiethnic students in East San Jose, we began to pray again to discern how to do this. We realized that not only were we going to cross a cultural barrier, but a social one as well. Using the normal methods of traditional evangelism would probably have been only marginally effective. While the gospel message always remains the same, the method of communication must be contextualized to those who would receive it. Interacting with our student leaders told us that theology and doctrine were going to be less important than earthy testimonies and hard-hitting messages. We also discovered the importance of the arts in communicating the gospel message. While Asian churches emphasize academia in their communication, multiethnic students were touched by music, poetry, paintings, and rap. Their tastes might have been a little different, but artistic expression was previously missing from our ministry.

In terms of attendance, while S.O.U.L. averaged fifty to seventy kids during the school year, on our anniversary meetings, we would stuff 700-1,000 people into our church sanctuary. By the time of the second anniversary, we caught a glimpse of the impact of this ministry. The S.O.U.L. Second Anniversary program lasted four hours, but no one complained about the length. There were rap artists, deejays and poets. If anyone decided to go outside for a break, they would walk past paintings expressing spirituality and praises to God. The colors were bright and bold and communicated a message. When M.C. Hammer got up to speak, his message was on repentance and reconciliation, challenging the audience to get things right with God. He didn't mince words, but nobody was offended since they trusted him. Many responded to his call for salvation.

The most frequent dilemma that we had to tackle with S.O.U.L. was how to integrate them into the church body. While it wasn't uncommon to see some of the church kids at the S.O.U.L. meetings as word got out, trying to integrate non-Chinese streetwise urban-type kids into an upper middle class Chinese church was a daunting task. It was like trying to mix oil and water—they just didn't mix very easily. Tuesday nights were free flowing while Sunday mornings were structured. Tuesday nights included real stories about real people; Sunday mornings had traditional preaching. Tuesday nights were attended by

East Side students; Sunday mornings were predominantly West Side students. Tuesday nights were multiethnic; Sunday mornings was overwhelmingly Chinese.

Whatever happened to S.O.U.L.? It no longer exists. S.O.U.L. was changed to a Sunday afternoon worship service in order to invite older high school and college students from the church to join it. But things were different: the style was more church-like; the leadership was more traditional; and those who came were from a mixture of churched backgrounds and urban street culture. Over the course of a year, interest and attendance dwindled. Finally, the service was discontinued. In retrospect, it would have been better to allow S.O.U.L. to continue on Tuesday nights and develop it as a midweek multicultural worship service.

There is a tendency in Asian church culture to move everyone inward, and demonstrate unity by doing things together. As many Asian churches start English-speaking worship services, they require the English congregation to do certain things with the Chinese side of the church to maintain a sense of unity. It might be monthly joint worship services, or requiring identical programs—same message, same hymns, and same announcements, just in different languages. These practices are enforced in the name of church unity. The reasoning is that if we could all be in the same room together doing the same things, then we have unity in the church. The irony is that this is never taught in the Bible. Ephesians 4:3 teaches us, "Make every effort to keep the unity of the Spirit through the bond of peace." Unity is not something that we manufacture; it is something that we keep. Later on in verse 13, it says, "… until we all reach unity in the faith and in the knowledge of the Son of God and become mature, attaining to the whole measure of the fullness of Christ." Biblical unity is based on our faith and what we believe, not on what we do to keep everyone together in the same room.

The biblical mandate upon the church is not so much to keep it together as it is to send it out. When the early church laid hands upon Barnabas and Saul in Acts 13, there were no complaints about disrupting unity. They sent the two men out because they knew that was what God wanted them to do. Their unity was in their faith and that the gospel message was meant to be shared with others. When we asked the S.O.U.L. students to change their meeting time, we were responding to our cultural biases rather than a biblical mandate. There is something joyful in seeing believers from different cultural backgrounds gathering together on occasion. It reassures our common faith to worship together, but to ask one group to permanently conform to the styles and customs of another group stifles their ability to reach out to their community. Some of the church kids and some of the S.O.U.L. kids loved to get together at outreach events, camps and retreats, but if we had asked our church kids to switch to S.O.U.L., we would have hindered the original youth group as well. If we are to have a greater influence with the gospel, it comes from multiplying ministries, not from consolidation.

WHAT DOES THIS MEAN FOR ASIAN CHURCHES?

Should every Asian church in America try to duplicate multicultural ministry as it happened at the San Jose Chinese Alliance Church? Absolutely not! The calling and anointing that the Holy Spirit places upon a church is unique to that congregation. There is no need for another church to copy that anointing unless God has touched them with a similar call. However, every church does have a call to the Great Commission. For SJCAC, it was to reach multiethnic students in East San Jose. For another group it might mean reaching Caucasian friends of your church kids. For a church in New York Chinatown, it could mean crossing back over a cultural barrier to reach immigrant students in the neighborhood.

It all starts with praying for a vision to reach a group of students that are not like the ones you have now. They might be different ethnically or in social status. They might live near your church, but be of a different cultural identity. What is important is that they are peers of your youth group students. They know each other in school or the neighborhood. Your students will have regular and normal contact with them.

Once that is discerned, then you need to ask God for a student leader who has a passion to reach that group. It is likely that such a person is not in your leadership group today. At SJCAC, that person was Jason Ma. He had leadership ability, but was an outsider; yet full of passion. And he belonged to the community that the Holy Spirit was leading us to reach. At this point, passion and identity are far more important than biblical literacy. You can disciple a student and teach him the Bible, but it's much harder to infuse passion and impossible to create identity.

Next, you have to help that student recruit others to form a ministry team. An interesting phenomenon from the S.O.U.L. story is that three of the original five members of their ministry team had never been involved in youth group leadership. Two of them had never shown any interest before, but the S.O.U.L. idea sparked something in their spirit. God raised them up as student leaders and eventually, all of them went on to Bible colleges. One graduated from seminary, another is in process, and a third is in the preparation phase. Your student leaders need people around them who are equally passionate about reaching the students God has assigned to you. They won't go far alone. When they have others around them, it will encourage them to push through numerous obstacles, while at the same time providing partners in prayer, accountability, and growth.

We also discovered how important it was to have a significant church leader who would champion our ministry. In our case, it was Rev. Abraham Poon, the church's senior pastor. We could not have asked God for a better person to give credibility to what we were doing. Once it was obvious that Rev. Poon not only was willing to allow S.O.U.L. to continue, but also to give his wholehearted endorsement, many potential roadblocks were removed. The champion of the ministry does not necessarily have to be the senior pastor, but it does have to be a person who is well-respected in the church. This leader should be able to rally support for a new ministry. Most churches tend to remain as they are; very few ministries seek radical change for themselves. A leader has to convince them that this new ministry may be God's will for their church.

Youth pastors, and especially volunteer youth workers, are usually near the bottom of the ranking order when it comes to giving direction to a church. If we are unable to convince church leaders that a new youth group is a good idea, it doesn't mean that we are poor leaders or that church members are bad people. We simply need an advocate who can speak out for the new cause and has the trust of parents. They may not agree with the new cause, but they're willing to listen to the advocate, and perhaps, agree to allow the project to continue.

FOR SUCH A TIME AS THIS

Those of us who are leading youth in Asian churches need to take a few steps back and get a broader view of the ministry landscape for today. It is time for us to take risks. The Asian church needs to take radical steps to move our ministries forward. In the latter part of the twentieth century, most of the emphasis on English-speaking ministries was directed at adults. This is understandable, but I also believe it is a great strategic error. Most of the adult ministries were focused inwardly because people believed their needs were not being met. So when congregations were being formed or churches planted, most of the focus was on providing ministry for those who were already saved in the kingdom of God. It took so much to do this that there was little time to think about evangelism or reaching an entirely new people group.

Youth ministry could stay the same, but it could be so radically different. Certainly, youth workers can get bogged down just paying attention to church kids, but teens are so much easier to change than adults. They are not as concerned about their own spiritual needs as their parents might be. It is not difficult to find junior high or high school students who are willing to take on a new challenge in ministry. Many of them are tired of the same old things happening. If there is hope of a ministry with the potential to have a real impact in another person's life, you can count on these students joining in.

Many of our students at SJCAC lamented that they could not comfortably bring friends to church who were not Chinese. They enjoyed what we were doing in our youth program, but they knew that their lives at church were somewhat cut off from the real world. They lived in neighborhoods and went to school with friends from other ethnic groups. Then, on weekends, they were suddenly thrust into this Asian bubble when they came to our youth group and worship services. Church life and school life did not intersect.

We are living in an era in which the Holy Spirit is doing surgery on the Asian church. It involves more than just the way we look and the way we conduct our ministry. The fruit that is being borne is going to look different. We are not going to be satisfied just having good students with 4.0 GPA's. We will be producing young men and women who will take Christ's Great Commission seriously. They are not going to limit themselves to 4.2% of our nation's population. Our students will open their eyes and see fields that are white for harvest. They will realize that they have access to a multiethnic community. More importantly, they will see open doors into other communities. They will realize that the favor of God is resting on them and that they have been appointed for such a time as this to reach the nations with the gospel of Jesus Christ.

They need help. Our students need youth pastors and adult leaders who can see what God is revealing. We are in the position to empower and commission our students to become the seeds of revival that will move the Asian church to a greater role in fulfilling the Great Commission. It is a movement that will not stop with Asian churches. It is a revival that could potentially impact all of America and to the ends of the earth.

Oh, by the way, about a year after S.O.U.L. was birthed, our church voted to change its name to the San Jose CHRISTIAN Alliance Church. Who says, "Youth ministries can't influence their churches?"

NOTES

[1] Barna Research Group, www.barna.org, 2004.

[2] Robert L. Niklaus, *All For Jesus* (Nyack, NY: The Christian and Missionary Alliance, 1986), 87-89.

[3] Dann Spader, *The Sonlife Strategy* (Elburn, IL: Sonlife Ministries, 1998), 7.

[4] Terrance J. Reeves and Claudette E. Bennett, *We the People: Asians in the U.S., Census 2000 Special Reports* (U.S. Census Bureau, 2000).

9

Incarnational Ministry for Asian Youth

Brian Hall and Cheryl Seid

This chapter presents a distinct parachurch ministry perspective, yet a compelling explanation for why they do what they do. Brian and Cheryl are part of Young Life, and they use creative ways of Christian outreach for those who aren't being reached by traditional church ministries. I hope their examples will spark your creativity in ministering beyond the church walls.

A significant find in a study of religious affiliation in the United States is that Asian adolescents—when compared to whites, blacks and Latinos—are the most unchurched racial/ethnic group of teenagers in the nation. According to the survey, *more than half* of all Asian high school kids in America have either *no* religious belief or practice a *non-Christian* religion.[1] A 1997 survey of Chinese freshmen at Rutgers University revealed similar findings: a whopping 48 percent of Chinese American freshmen had no religious belief.[2] In America, such a high level of religious disaffiliation within a particular ethnic group is rare and makes Asian Americans unusually likely candidates for conversion to a religion later in life.[3]

According to sociologists Rodney Stark and Roger Finke, "[T]he single most unstable 'religion' of origin" is "no religion"[4]—when people *lack* commitments to a particular religious orientation, they are much *more* likely to eventually join a new religious group. This suggests that Asian youth represent an untouched "harvest field" for Christian ministry. This is NOT because Asian young people have *rejected* Christianity, per se; more likely than not, they simply have not been *introduced* to Christianity. Furthermore, even in cases where Asian young people may have been introduced to Christianity, it is often done so in an environment that gives them a very limited (and perhaps distorted) view of Christianity, one in which the Christian religion is often seen as just another thing to do—as something that is done on Sundays at church—rather than as a way of living that adds to and affects all other areas of their life.

These studies point to a growing need to develop stronger evangelism strategies for reaching Asian teens. Sadly, few churches—Asian and non-Asian alike—make evangelistic outreach a high priority in their ministries. As Doug Fields (youth pastor for the popular Saddleback Church in California) laments, evangelism is "a weakly expressed program in many youth ministries," noting that "it is difficult to fulfill on a program level" and "threatening on a personal level."[5] More often than not, most church ministries—especially those in Asian church settings—tend to focus primarily on the discipleship of young people raised in the church and on "fellowship." The reasons for this are complex and may be due, in part, to the lack of significance attributed to youth ministry in many Asian churches and the failure to see such ministry as more than just—as some have described—a "babysitting service."[6]

This is where methods developed by Young Life could play a vital role in helping youth workers to impact Asian teenagers for many years to come. For more than 60 years, Young Life has been pioneering the concept of "incarnational ministry" with teenagers, where caring Christian adults go into the world of teenagers and live among them, developing unconditional, no-strings-attached relationships that model the Gospel both in action and in words. According to Young Life founder, Jim Rayburn, the "winning and establishing of a soul for Jesus Christ cannot be done on a hit-and-run basis."[7] This biblically-based, relational approach to evangelism has enabled Young Life leaders to introduce the Christian faith to thousands of teenagers from many diverse backgrounds and from around the world. Simply put, instead of expecting nonreligious kids to come to church, our leaders basically take "the church" to them. Such an approach is necessary, says Rayburn, because most young people—Asians included—are "not being touched by any other methods."[8]

Young Life began its evangelistic outreach to teenagers in 1941, focusing initially on American teenagers in the suburbs, most of whom were white. Since then, the mission has expanded its goal to reach "every kid" for Jesus Christ—black kids, Hispanic kids, kids in the city, kids with disabilities, teenage mothers, kids in foreign countries and, yes, Asian kids. Our recently implemented "Asian Initiative" is a campaign to recruit adults to Young Life who have a heart for reaching non-Christian Asian American kids and to partner with and assist Asian churches that have a burden to give evangelism a greater priority in their youth ministries. In both New Jersey and California, we have established specialized Young Life ministries that focus primarily on Asian American teens. While Asian youth are similar to other teens in many ways, there are cultural nuances that need to be considered when reaching out to Asian youth. This chapter will examine two problems we observed while doing outreach in traditional Asian youth ministry settings, and we will introduce two methods used in Young Life that may help.

PROBLEM 1: LACK OF ADULT INTERACTION WITH ASIAN TEENS

In Tim Smith's book *The Seven Cries of Today's Teens*, the author notes that many teenagers these days are "growing up alone" and that their lives are "devoid of any meaningful interaction with adults." Although adults may assume that teenagers want to be left alone, in actuality many teenagers desire "meaningful conversation" and interaction with parents and other adults.[9] This problem was eloquently expressed by Young Life's founder Jim Rayburn a number of years ago when he said that young people "are waiting for somebody to care about them enough . . . to bridge this tragic and terrible gap that exists in our culture between teenagers and adults."[10] Sadly, this "tragic and terrible gap" that exists between teenagers and adults seems to carry over into many Asian church youth ministries as well.

From our conversations with many Asian church youth pastors and from our interactions with Asian congregations, we find that youth ministry in general is given "low status" in many Asian churches. Oftentimes, the so-called "youth ministry" in such churches is run by parents who—though well-intentioned—lack any special training in youth ministry or by seminary students and interns, many of whom may view their time in youth ministry as temporary and merely a training ground for other, more "significant" future ministries (e.g., senior pastor, church planter, foreign missionary, etc.). There is a serious shortage of adults in Asian churches who are committed to serving Asian youth as a full-time lifelong vocation. For those adults who do serve at least temporarily in Asian youth ministry, the focus seems to be on the discipleship of kids who are already Christians and/or who have been raised in the church. In light of the short-term tenure of many Asian youth ministry leaders, it is unlikely that most adult leaders have much time in their schedules to also devote to interaction with and evangelization of kids outside of the church.

Consider the following hypothetical scenario of a seminary student studying for an M.Div. degree with the hopes of eventually starting a church of his own. This adult has been appointed to oversee the youth ministry of a particular Asian church. Since he attends a seminary that is a one-hour drive from the church and because he is carrying a full academic load, he can work at the church only on weekends. This youth pastor runs the church's youth group meetings on Friday nights and assists with the church's Sunday school classes on Sunday mornings. On Sunday afternoon, he returns to the seminary, where he will then spend Sunday through Friday concentrating on his studies. Even if the youth pastor in this hypothetical example can squeeze time into his schedule to interact with church kids, he will still probably have no time left to spend with non-Christian kids outside of the church. The youth pastor may try to get around this by telling the Christian kids in the church that it is *their* job to reach out to their non-Christian peers, but unless he and other adult leaders actively model how to do this, such advice may fall on deaf ears. One reason that few kids in Asian churches engage in incarnational-style, relationship-based evangelism is because their leaders are not engaging in incarnational-style, relationship-based evangelism. "Anything difficult—like evangelism—usually has to be pushed by leadership," notes Doug Fields. Only if kids "see evangelism modeled by their leaders and diligently taught from Scripture" will they "gradually understand its purpose and make it a priority."[11]

The absence of adult involvement in kids' lives means that teenagers in many Asian church youth ministries rarely see their leaders outside of formal church programs and, therefore, lack adult role models who show how the Christian life is to be lived *outside* of the church. For such kids, their Christian faith is typically confined to church and church activities with little or no impact on lives outside of the church. This is especially unfortunate in light of the fact that there are still "too many unreached teenagers" for whom something needs to be done so that they can hear "the good news of Jesus Christ."[12]

PROBLEM 2: LACK OF EVANGELISTIC-ORIENTED PROGRAMMING

In addition to the lack of adult involvement in the lives of kids, another reason for the struggle with outreach involves the program itself. If evangelism does take place in the Asian church, it usually happens as an "event," as something that kids do when they pass out pamphlets at a mall or when they hold a once-a-year "coffeehouse" or "seeker night" at youth group (which ofttimes attracts more Christian kids than non-Christians). When forced to find new ways to reach non-Christian kids, many frustrated adults complain that they barely have enough time to minister to the kids already in the church or they point out that they don't know any other way to reach non-Christian Asians other than to duplicate what they have been doing for years. Thus, it just becomes easier to focus on "fellowship."

Occasionally, youth leaders in Asian churches do attempt to make their youth programs more sensitive and inviting to non-Christian teenagers, but they usually do so in the context of the ministry programs that they already have in place. For example, they might run a Friday night meeting that contains a seeker-oriented skit. The rest of the meeting, however, may still consist of a blend of worship music, preaching, Bible study, and prayer, elements that may not be conducive to reaching non-Christian Asian teenagers.

If the goal of a program is evangelism, then it must be wholly catered to the non-Christian Asian whom the program is trying to reach. One of the important points that Doug Fields makes is that different programs or meetings should be designed for different target audiences and that sometimes Christian kids need to be reminded that evangelistic programs are "not for [them]."[13]

A SOLUTION: CONTACT WORK AND CLUB

Young Life has been pioneering a number of methods that have enabled thousands of unchurched teenagers to be introduced to the Christian faith. Two methods that may be particularly fitting in the Asian community are what we call *contact work* and *club*.

CONTACT WORK

At the heart of the Young Life mission is an adult who cares about kids and willing to build relationships with teenagers. Young Life calls this "contact work," the development of lasting one-on-one adult friendships with teens in order to earn the right to verbally and non-verbally share the Gospel of Jesus Christ. Contact work is "the foundational principle behind Young Life's ability to communicate the Gospel to disinterested kids," and it is "the platform from which uncommitted adolescents can experience the Gospel."[14] Young Life leaders are inspired in this task by imitating the model of Jesus Christ Himself, who—according to John 1:14—left the comforts of heaven and became a human being to live among the people with whom He was sent to minister, or as *The Message* so eloquently puts it, "The Word became flesh and blood, and moved into the neighborhood." Young Life is about "moving into the neighborhood" of teenagers so that teenagers can see Jesus Christ lived out in the lives of adult leaders. It has been said that a more appropriate term for "contact work" may actually be "Christian leadership."[15] This is because Young Life leaders move into the neighborhood of the adolescent subculture in order to lead kids to Jesus Christ, taking their cues from Paul when he wrote: "You paid careful attention to the way we lived among you, and determined to live that way yourselves. In imitating us, you imitated the Master." (1 Thessalonians 1:5-6, *The Message*) Contact work is essentially Christian leadership by example.

More descriptively, contact work means that adult leaders meet Asian kids on their turf, go where they go, get involved in their activities, and take an interest in them. In other words, a Young Life leader establishes "contact" with an Asian American high school kid. This "contact" can take place anywhere: at a local high school, on a tennis court, at a shopping mall, at an orchestra concert, at Borders... basically, any place where Asian kids hang out. To show encouragement and support, a Young Life leader may also attend important sporting events and award ceremonies.

In an effort to do activities that may also receive parental support and approval, Young Life leaders may invite Asian kids to study with them at a library, and they may tutor them. In New Jersey, the Young Life leaders have talked about opening an SAT review center. In California, they take kids on a college tour as well as on an annual trip to Japan. None of these activities are religious, per se, but what they do provide are opportunities for adult leaders to get to know and build relationships with Asian American teens. Furthermore, they provide secular Asian American kids an opportunity to see how Christian adults interact with the world and deal with the pressures of daily life.

Young Life has categorized the various dimensions of contact work into three levels: 1) "being seen," 2) "conversing," and 3) "enjoying activities together." The first level—*being seen*—basically means that an adult leader is seen at the events important in an Asian teenager's life. It is important for a leader seeking to build friendships with a teenager "to express his or her interest by attending events which are important to the teenager."[16] We have observed that at many school events, such as tennis matches and band concerts, Asian parents are often not in attendance, leading some Asian kids to feel that their parents are never there for them.[17] Some parents say they don't have the time; others don't regard these activities as important. Whatever the reason, leaders can have a huge impact on Asian kids simply by showing up at these events and being seen, filling the role that should be done by Asian parents but, sadly, often is not. The next level—*conversing*—requires that the leader open up a channel of communication with Asian kids to talk about life, their feelings, and other things. "Real friendships can be built only through communication, and this communication must be more than an occasional 'Hi!'"[18] The final level—*enjoying activities together*—"is the finest way to get to know a young person."[19] Doing activities with a young person helps to solidify the relationship and enables adults to truly become friends with their teenage counterparts.

Leaders develop relationships with young people "for the same reason that Christ came to humanity: to reveal God with no strings attached."[20] Over time, it is hoped that these interactions will evolve into unconditional friendships between the Young Life leader and the young people with whom he or she has contact. As these friendships mature, it is further hoped that the leader will "win the right to be heard"; the right to offer advice and insight to his or her teenage friends. It is when these preconditions are established that Young Life leaders achieve an openness of heart in their teenage friends to share the Gospel. Some of these young people may eventually get involved in a Young Life group, but many do not. That's OK because the goal of contact work is not to draw kids to our meetings; the goal is simply to model God's love and be there for kids, as ambassadors of Christ. Even kids who never get involved in a Young Life group recognize their local leader as an adult figure they can trust and can turn to in times of need. We desire that by doing incarnational ministry with teenagers, we can show them Jesus Christ.

CLUB

Young Life has created a unique seeker-oriented outreach meeting that is designed with non-Christians in mind but also with Christian kids in mind as a place where they can invite their non-Christian friends. "Club" is the name Young Life gives to its weekly outreach meetings. Sometimes described as "organized chaos," club typically takes place at the home of one of the teenagers involved in Young Life or in a community center or some other neutral, preferably non-church setting. The goal is to create a positive atmosphere in which non-Christian kids feel welcome and appreciated. Doug Fields notes, "Until students are environmentally comfortable, they won't be theologically aware."[21] In Young Life, we follow Paul's example of relating to all kinds of people when he said "I have become all things to all men so that by all possible means I might save some." (1 Corinthians 9:22) The result is a high energy, fast-paced meeting geared almost entirely to non-Christian teenagers.

Anywhere from 30 to 100 kids (sometimes more) will show up for an hour of crazy skits, fun games, and the singing of popular secular songs as well as hits from the past. Club is carefully planned so that it never runs over an hour. After club, the leaders and kids may go out to eat, watch a movie, or do some other fun activity as a group. For many kids, club is the highlight of their week. A typical club consists of four elements: (1) music, (2) minutes (or games), (3) announcements, and (4) the message.

For music in Young Life clubs, we lead kids in singing primarily secular songs by artists like U2, John Mayer, and even The Beatles. In addition to singing songs popular on MTV or on their iPods, Young Life also tries to find songs with meaningful words that will resonate with the young people in attendance, many of whom do not have a relationship with Jesus Christ, songs like Simple Plan's "Welcome to My Life" or Avril Lavigne's "Complicated." We also use songs that may be especially appropriate to Asian teens, songs that deal with pressure to succeed, not feeling accepted, and family issues. Although dated, a classic song like "Cat's In the Cradle," for example, can still speak powerfully to kids struggling with relationships with their fathers. Overall, good singing "can be a tremendous asset to the meeting's atmosphere and effectiveness."[22] The goal of singing is to bring kids together and help prepare them for the message.

The purpose of the minutes (or games) is simply to provide kids an opportunity to laugh. As Doug Fields observes, having a good time at a Christian gathering "is one of the most powerful ways to shatter the *boring* stereotype."[23] We see the minutes as "an important ingredient for breaking down barriers and making kids laugh and relax in a happy setting."[24] When doing games, we typically select kids who are comfortable up front without their prior knowledge. This creates an element of surprise among the kids as they nervously wonder who will be called up front and also prevents the meeting from dragging, which sometimes happens when a leader must ask for volunteers. The announcements are brief (two to three minutes) and are used to welcome kids to club and to highlight one or two activities going on.

The last ten to fifteen minutes of club consist of the message, a brief talk given by a Young Life leader on some aspect of God and His relevance in kids' lives. The message is usually highly personal and is effective at connecting with kids who may not normally think about faith issues. Young Life leaders do not necessarily explain the entire Gospel story at one meeting, nor do they initiate "altar calls." Although skeptics may look at the message delivered at club and wonder why Young Life leaders do not give "altar calls" or employ other evangelistic techniques at their club meetings, the reason is quite clear: Young Life is about relationships, not emotionally charged responses to the Gospel. Young Life uses the message as a springboard for further discussions about Christianity. Suppose that a non-Christian teenager attends club for his or her first time. After the meeting, a leader or one of the mature Christian kids in the club can use what was discussed in the message as a topic of conversation with the non-Christian young person. "What did you think of what the speaker said tonight?", "Do you ever feel the way that he does?" and so forth. It is hoped that having these kinds of introspective conversations can lead to deeper and more meaningful discussions on faith, all done in the context of relationships.

Although the music and style of club has changed since the early days of Young Life, for us club remains "the most effective setting for the proclamation of the Gospel" and "a highly effective tool in reaching out to the majority of a targeted adolescent community."[25]

INCARNATIONAL MINISTRY TO ASIAN YOUTH

All kids—regardless of race or ethnicity—want to be loved and know that someone cares for them.[26] The goal of the "Asian Initiative" in Young Life is to fine-tune the well-established tools, principles, and resources of Young Life to offer Asian kids a new perspective on life. Pastor Ken Fong notes that all "human beings are governed by certain social structures," structures that can be "utilized to win many new people to Christ."[27] In other words, we must use "methods that match people," with the realization that "certain approaches to delivering the good news are more effective than others."[28] We believe that by focusing our attention on Asian kids, we will draw kids who would never step foot into a Young Life club if it did not have the word "Asian" in its name. Asian kids want to find a place where they feel comfortable, a place where they feel "at home."

For example, in most of the suburban schools in New Jersey, Asians are always in the minority, like in many parts of the United States. But watch how an Asian kid comes to life in a room with other Asians, kids who know what it's like to be required to take piano and violin lessons, to go to Chinese or Korean school on the weekends, to eat rice at every meal... and sadly, to also be laughed at or teased because of their race. We don't want to exaggerate stereotypes, but many Asian kids have said that they feel a special bond with other Asians who understand these unique cultural experiences. The goal of the Asian Initiative in Young Life is to be sensitive to these experiences and to celebrate these differences as another means of reaching kids.

This is important, especially in light of the fact that many Asian kids say that they have an extremely difficult time relating with their parents and other adults, sometimes because of language differences, other times because of cultural traditions that discourage openness and visible forms of emotional sharing. A trained Young Life or youth leader, on the other hand, may be able to open previously closed doors of communication and support to an Asian kid, perhaps with even more profound results than a leader who does ministry predominantly with white kids. Hopefully, in the process, we can help Asian kids develop stronger relationships not only with God but with their parents as well.

Respecting the teenagers' relationship to their parents is crucial. Parent-to-staff relationships are important in building long-term trust. This respect is demonstrated through home visits and phone calls with parents. To show care and affirmation, a Young Life leader may nurture teens as surrogate parents. Many Asian teens are not accustomed to physical touch (hugs, pats on back, etc.) and verbally expressing emotions. We exemplify this to them in an appropriate manner.

The Young Life ministry principles can be summarized as follows:

- Go where Asian kids congregate
- Accept Asian kids as they are and with no strings attached
- Build on kids' instinct for adventure
- Learn how to walk in wisdom and respect with those outside the Christian faith
- Recognize the dignity of each person
- Expect to earn the right to be heard
- Find a neutral setting to meet together
- Create an environment that is casual and non-threatening
- Capitalize on the elements of good humor and music to establish an openness of mind and heart
- Consider it a sin to bore kids, especially with the Gospel of Jesus Christ
- Speak naturally and conversationally, and in terms familiar to a teenager's vocabulary
- Communicate our enthusiasm and certainties, rather than flaunt our doubts
- Affirm Asian kids' individual and cultural identities

Reaching non-Christian Asian American kids is the heartbeat of Young Life's Asian Initiative. We follow the example of Jesus Christ to go into the world of teenagers and live among them, developing unconditional relationships that model the Gospel. Through methods like contact work and club, we are reaching Asian teens in fun and non-threatening ways. We invite those who share a similar burden to join us. We would love to partner with Asian churches that have a heart for evangelism so that together we may reach the surrounding communities that need to experience the love of God.

NOTES

[1] Barry A. Kosmin and Seymour P. Lachman, *One Nation Under God: Religion in Contemporary American Society* (New York: Harmony Books, 1993).

[2] Cooperative Institutional Research Program (CIRP), *Cooperative Institutional Research Program Data for Rutgers University–New Brunswick* (New Brunswick, NJ: Rutgers Office of Institutional Research, 1997).

[3] Brian Hall, "Social and Cultural Contexts in Conversion to Christianity Among Chinese American College Students," *Sociology of Religion* 67:2 (2006), 131-147.

[4] Rodney Stark and Roger Finke, *Acts of Faith: Explaining the Human Side of Religion* (Berkeley, CA: University of California Press, 2000), 121.

[5] Doug Fields, *Purpose-Driven Youth Ministry: 9 Essential Foundations for Healthy Growth* (Grand Rapids: Zondervan, 1998), 47.

[6] Victor Quon, "Do We Really Believe the Great Commission?" *Asian American Youth Ministry* (Washington, DC: L^2 Foundation, 2006), 82.

[7] Jim Rayburn, "The Heart of the Mission," *Young Life – Leadership I & II* (Colorado Springs, CO: Young Life), YLM-3.

[8] Ibid.

[9] Timothy Smith, *The Seven Cries of Today's Teens* (Nashville: Integrity, 2003), 197.

[10] Young Life website, <http://www.younglife.org>.

[11] Fields, 109.

[12] Ibid., 88.

[13] Fields, 111.

[14] Neil Atkinson and Dick Langford, "Signature of Young Life – Contact Work," *Young Life – Leadership I & II* (Colorado Springs, CO: Young Life), FYL-3.

[15] Ibid.

[16] Ibid., FYL-5.

[17] Jeanette Yep, "Your Parents Love You, My Parents Love Me," *Following Jesus Without Dishonoring Your Parents* (Downers Grove, IL: InterVarsity Press, 1998), 36.

[18] Atkinson and Langford, FYL-5.

[19] Ibid.

[20] Ibid., FYL-3.

[21] Fields, 117.

[22] Fil Anderson, "The Traditional Young Life Club," *Young Life – Leadership I & II* (Colorado Springs, CO: Young Life), FYL-63.

[23] Fields, 120.

[24] Anderson, FYL-63.

[25] Anderson, FYL-61.

[26] Smith, 47-62.

[27] Ken Uyeda Fong, *Pursuing the Pearl: A Comprehensive Resource for Multi-Asian Ministry* (Valley Forge, PA: Judson Press, 1999), 5.

[28] Ibid., 75.

10

From Church Pew to Red Light District: Empowering Youth to Fight Social Injustices

Eugene S. Kim

I had first read about this youth group through a printed newsletter from International Justice Mission, catching my attention because Asian youth groups are rarely highlighted as an example for others in the area of social justice. I was compelled to find out what God was doing in their midst. But before you read further, I should caution you with a disclaimer of sorts, something like a parental advisory for shocking content. While there aren't explicit lyrics, the description of evils in the world is nothing short of disturbing. The response by this youth group is simply bold and inspiring, and I hope, contagious for raising a generation that will dream big dreams.

Got any problems? Sure, we all do! How about your youth? Do they have problems? Your youth are often dealing with adult-sized issues, but with an adolescent perspective. So why on earth would we want to introduce such a huge challenge like social injustice to our youth groups especially when it is seemingly outside their power, grasp, and reason to do anything about it? Because the Scriptures plainly exhort: "...learn to do right! Seek justice, encourage the oppressed. Defend the cause of the fatherless, plead the case of the widow..." (Isaiah 1:17)

Let's imagine introducing the problem of oppression to our youth. What is oppression? Oppression is the arbitrary and cruel exercise of power, the forceful removal of human rights through means of coercion and force. Oppression can take a number of various forms, ranging from extortion to slavery to false imprisonment to forced prostitution. Let's be more specific and talk about the forced prostitution of child slaves.

Forced prostitution is considered to be a severe form of trafficking in persons. Many of these enslaved prostitutes are mere adolescents and even children as young as five years of age. Their bodies are sometimes violated up to thirty times a day. Their payment, if they are paid at all, cannot keep them out of their burgeoning debt imposed by their oppressors.

Imagine how your youth would respond to such an atrocity. Perhaps there would be an initial interest: "Wow, can't believe this stuff is happening today."; "That's really sad and depressing."; "There are millions of children forced into this stuff? I feel sick."; "There are some evil people out there."; "I'm sure glad that's not happening to me."; "Can we do anything about it?"

Once your students gain a scope of a specific problem, reality may sink in and your youth may then feel an immense sense of hopelessness: "What a huge problem!"; "What am I supposed to do with this information?"; "I'm powerless."; "I'm just a high school kid. What can I do living here in the U.S.?"; "Like I need another thing to worry about in my life."; "Where is God in all of this?"; "This is an adult-sized problem and I'm just a kid."

Oops. Maybe we shouldn't have shared anything at all. Perhaps the adage, "ignorance is bliss" is all too true. I don't think so.

IGNORANCE IS NOT BLISS

Gary Haugen, the founder of International Justice Mission, states, "Most of us have seen something of this ugliness in dark, vague images on the news. Sooner or later, these images come home to all of us, and at some point they descend upon our young people. The question is: What do we offer them? A remote control to change the channel? An up-tempo praise song or a useless sense of guilt? I think we need to offer them the God of justice and the opportunity to actually do something."[1]

In doing so, we are revealing to our youth the other side of oppression and its atrocious acts. Namely, that Jesus Christ is building His kingdom and He is willing to use ordinary Christians to perform God-sized miracles of rescue and redemption. How much more important is it to invite Christian youth into this endeavor! The future lies with them as well as the faith and courage needed to make a change. Today's Asian American youth are faithful, courageous, resourceful, and seek out "a grander purpose beyond suburban safety and a gray twilight that knows no authentic victory or defeat." Our youth need to be aware of the heinous brutality and unspeakable oppression that people suffer in our world. They must hear it from a Christian worldview because the story doesn't end with people's suffering, but rather with God's finished plan of rescue and redemption. They must hear it, and as fellow youth workers and pastors, they must hear it from you.

THE GAME PLAN

The purpose of this chapter is to outline a few principles that will introduce a plan of outreach to the needy for your youth group. By no means will I be able to cover all the points necessary to help youth groups be challenged toward outreach, but I will include some strategies used in developing our campaign called, "Raise 100 to Free 100." This campaign, which began in February of 2004, is student-initiated and the goal is to raise $100,000 for the purpose of helping the International Justice Mission free one hundred children from forced prostitution. The campaign required us to develop four key strategies.

1. STRIKING A CHORD

"Will you please close your eyes and bow your heads? I would like for you to envision a young child who you love dearly Imagine a girl. She could be your younger sister, or cousin, or a child that you've befriended in the children's ministry here in church. What's her name? How old is she? Do you see the joy in her eyes and the warmth of her laughter? What fond memories do you have?

Now imagine that she has suddenly disappeared. She's been abducted. Where has she gone? You discover that she's been taken to a brothel in another city to be sold for sex with strange adult men—sometimes five, ten, fifteen, thirty times a day If this child you are thinking of doesn't listen to her abductor's wishes, she will be cruelly beaten She's only fed once a day. Very little of the money that she earns for her abductor would be seen by this child.

What would you do? Would you call the police? Would you dial 911? Would you get angry? Would you demand justice? Well, what if the very police and government officials that should be protecting our children are actually protecting this type of operation, and are even customers of these brothels? Now what would you do? Who would you turn to? Is there any hope? If you could do anything within your power to stop this, would you do it? (Pause...)

OK, you can open your eyes now. What I just shared with you is NOT a myth or a fictitious story. This is a reality for hundreds of thousands of children all over the world. We are talking about children as young as five-years-old that are being kidnapped, taken to unfamiliar city or country, and raped over and over again for the profit of evil, greedy people. If you could do something to stop this atrocity, would you?"[2]

Youth today may appear to be apathetic and self-absorbed, but you know what happens when you strike a chord that is important to them. Talk about their favorite band, someone they like, a tripped-out ride, child prostitution, Abercrombie and Fitch, shaved ice or Starbucks and they go nuts! Wait a minute, did someone mention child prostitution? Youth are amazed to think that if they lived in another part of the world, they could easily have been abducted, raped, and forced into prostitution. This includes both girls AND boys. Acts of injustice always strike a chord. Perhaps it's a God-given response knowing that injustice does not sit well with our God neither. When we hear stories of injustice, or unfairness, or of bullies beating up the little guy, it evokes a response... a reaction.

Introduce your students to the injustices in this world and see what happens. Make it a month-long study. Make your youth feel uncomfortable with the atrocities going on. Do not shelter them from the truth of how evil people are in this world. Inform them and do not sugar-coat what is happening to those who are oppressed. Show news clips, videos, movies, testimonies. Let it strike a chord.

You will get all kinds of reactions (and from their parents, but that's another chapter!). The students will want to know if you are being truthful. They will want to verify information. Some may begin to feel guilty. Others will feel hopeless. Some will feel sympathetic. Some won't care. A few will want to be useful. And then someone will begin to dream.

2. SMALL DREAMS DO NOT INFLAME THE HEARTS OF MEN

Proverbs 29:18 (NKJV) states, "Where there is no vision, the people perish." We need to instill in our youth dreams that are bigger than themselves. We should pray and hope that God gives our young people vision that is practical, realistic, and action-oriented. Something that our youth can fulfill knowing that it is God's destiny for their lives. Are we training and teaching our young people to be big dreamers OR are we developing pew warmers? Are we willing to break molds, including cultural limits and human expectations OR are we trying to fit our youth into molds pre-made before they were even conceived? What are we ultimately trying to do in our youth ministries?

Teach our youth to dream big because they have a big God. Yes, the reality is that our youth are limited and flawed, but look at what Jesus did with five loaves of bread and two fish given by a little boy (Luke 9:10-17). Nurture these dreams and pray over them. Invite others to be part of this dream. Bill Bright cautioned: "Small dreams do not inflame the hearts of men." Give them the resources needed to fulfill their dreams. Train them to multiply their passions by sharing their vision with others. Then watch and see what happens.

We also need to teach on the cost of pursuing our dreams; with any dream there is a sacrifice. In Genesis 13:10-18, Abraham faced alienation, physical pain, and disability because of his vision. It cost Paul imprisonment and torture (Acts 21:27). And for Jesus, it cost Him His life (Luke 23:46). John Maxwell noted: "A vision enables us to give up at any moment all that we are, so that we may become all that God wants us to become."

3. TEACH WHAT GOD HATES

God hates injustice and loves the needy. Scripture is full of claims regarding justice and compassion. The Bible talks much also about oppression, the word "oppression" is mentioned twenty times in Scripture; the word "oppressed" forty-seven times; and "justice" one hundred thirty-four times. Does God have something to say about justice and oppression? Yes. Do we as youth workers talk about it much? No. Why? Gary Haugen states, "Many who lack faith will shrink away from the distant, dark world of injustice. Still others will water down the Word and imagine that they can love God without loving their brother, or wanting to 'justify' themselves, they will invent elaborate quibbles with Jesus about who is and is not their neighbor."[1] Teach your youth about our God being big on justice. Teach your youth about the things God truly hates. Read on your own Proverbs 14:31, Psalm 146, Psalm 10, Matthew 12:9-21, Psalm 73, Psalm 9.

There are many good resources and Bible study material that can introduce you to this important topic and more importantly, about how God cares for it. Because our youth are generally visual learners, you should also check the various movies, websites and video clips that are out there.[3]

4. NEVER TOO YOUNG TO MAKE A DIFFERENCE

As youth workers, we should be in the "business" of helping children become adults—more specifically, God-fearing adults. God has placed us into the crucial years of a young person's life. Many decisions regarding life, faith, and career are being shaped with your input. We are not to make their decisions for them, but we are to direct them to their Maker, teaching them and discipling them through life's issues.

Part of doing our "job" well then, is enabling and empowering youth to eventually make adult decisions. Treat your youth as adults-in-the-making. Respect them and love them. Also realize within each youth, there is the potential to do great good (and unfortunately, great evil). We should always be mindful that we are there, alongside their parents, to mentor and coach them to make adult-sized decisions. They will eventually become fellow kingdom workers, missionaries, and dare I say, some who may take over your jobs!

When youth feel empowered and encouraged to make a difference, they will respond. Giving them authority to make real decisions that shape your youth group will demonstrate that you are serious about leadership development and seeing the next generation take charge. If you treat your youth as potential adults, they will start to head in that direction. If you don't, well then, let's just say you are relegating your crucial role of youth worker to "glorified baby-sitter" and move on. It is absolutely essential that we learn to empower them now. This type of ownership in the hands of creative, God-fearing "adults-in-the-making" is indeed a scary thing (in the eyes of Satan) and a wonderful thing (in the eyes of God). Paul said to Timothy, "Don't let anyone look down on you because you are young, but set an example for the believers in speech, in life, in love, in faith, and in purity" (1 Tim. 4:12).

CASE STUDY: "RAISE 100 TO FREE 100"

The "Raise 100 to Free 100" campaign is a student-initiated ministry here at Chinese Baptist Church of Orange County (CBCOC) that is committed to raising $100,000 to help free 100 young children from forced prostitution and sexual slavery. IJM can rescue a girl enslaved in forced prostitution for about $1,000. This campaign began with our introduction to curriculum provided by IJM (in partnership with Youth Specialties) titled "The Justice Mission" curriculum. This program is a video-enhanced youth curriculum reflecting the heart of God for the oppressed of the world, giving an inside look at the work of IJM, and showing the reality of injustice and what we could do about it.

Then we prayed. We prayed throughout the study series and for two weeks after the conclusion of the curriculum. What could one small youth group do to affect such a large problem? We asked ourselves, "Lord, what can we do?" The answer was, "Not much— by yourselves." But we also heard God say, "In Me, all things are possible."

Many students were repulsed and shocked by a Dateline NBC documentary (1/23/04) that was shown during youth group. It depicted how pedophiles in the U.S. would prey on children in foreign countries where governments are turning a blind eye. The suggestion came up to raise awareness and funds to rescue children from forced prostitution. The students decided to dream big. We only have "five loaves and two fish," but Christ simply asks, "Bring them here to me." The students began to offer what little they had and trusted in a big, big God.

Many students began contacting their friends, family, teachers, school officials, public officials, professional athletes and celebrities. Some students began going door-to-door in their neighborhoods, to local businesses, and to other churches. A PowerPoint presentation was made by students to introduce the topic of oppression and this campaign. A website was populated with information on social justice that could be downloaded.[4] Students were invited to attend other youth groups and make presentations to raise awareness of this atrocity and what students were willing to do in response.

Several fundraiser efforts conducted this past year include:

- Door-to-Door: Students went home-to-home to ask for donations.

- Letter Writing: Students wrote to their family and friends for donations.

- Loose Change: Our first fundraiser was to find loose change around their homes, closets, piggy banks, donating first from what we had.

- Snow Cones: During the summer, we purchased materials to sell shaved ice at church during the lunch hour and during Chinese School. We also asked for donations.

- Sponsored Car Wash: During the summer, we used some parking lot space to run a free carwash. The students received donations from sponsors (flat donation or per car rate) and from customers who had their cars washed.

- CBCOC's Blessings: Students made a presentation to the church and invited the church to consider supporting this cause through prayer and donations. In addition, CBCOC created a line item in their annual budget to receive and disperse donations on behalf of IJM.

- Lunch Fast: During the Retreat for Young Chinese Evangelicals (RYCE) 2004, our speaker challenged the RYCE students to fast once a week for a year. The money saved from fasting would then be donated to IJM.

- 30-Hour Famine: Two dozen students participated in a 30-Hour famine similar to what World Vision does. But the money raised and the cause communicated was for the fight against oppression.

- Inviting Other Youth Groups: Students prepared a 5-8 minute PowerPoint presentation to share the campaign with other youth groups. Through this effort, our funds raised doubled.

- Travel to Tier 2 Country: CBCOC has budgeted monies for a youth team to be sent summer of 2006 into a Tier 2 country, namely Thailand, Cambodia or India. The purpose will be to see firsthand rescued victims at rescue centers and to do prayer walks around red-light districts.

CONCLUSION

At the time of this writing, $33,298.80 has been raised through the "Raise 100 to Free 100" campaign. Praise the Lord!

Train your youth well. A motto we use in sharing what our youth group is about is "Love God and Love Others," based on the greatest commandment Jesus gave in Matthew 22:36-39. We usually do a great job of "Loving God," and most certainly, our ability to love others will be derived directly from our time experiencing God. But where in our youth groups do we love our neighbor—how do we, who have plenty, express love to the needy; we, who are free, relate to the oppressed; we, who are rich, show love to the poor? Micah 6:8 says: "He has showed you, O man, what is good. And what does the LORD require of you? To act justly and to love mercy and to walk humbly with your God." Open your youth to God's Word and the reality of the world and empower them to respond with great faith.

NOTES

[1] Jim Hancock, *The Justice Mission - A Video-Enhanced Curriculum Reflecting the Heart of God for the Oppressed of the World* (El Cajon, CA: Youth Specialties, 2002), p. 9.

[2] Excerpt from one of my youth's presentation given to the youth group at NewSong Church in Irvine, California.

[3] Recommended movies include: Hotel Rwanda (2004), The Agronomist (2003), Gandhi (1982), Schindler's List (1993), The Pianist (2002), Born Into Brothels: Calcutta's Red Light Kids (2004). International Justice Mission has many resources, including 2 informative videos: "Good News About Injustice" and "Children For Sale." You can order them online at: www.ijm.org

[4] The website for the "Raise 100 to Free 100" Campaign is at www.cbcoc.org/oppression —visit this website for additional resources.

11

Postmodern Principles for Asian American Youth Ministries

Joey Chen

One of the main challenges facing churches and ministries is figuring out how to understand the context in which we find ourselves. In America and around the world, we are increasingly influenced by postmodern thought. Changes have to be made to effectively bear witness to the gospel of Jesus Christ. This chapter provides a great introduction to what is happening and gives practical examples from the author's own experiences for engaging today's Asian American youth.

Postmodernism… the word itself raises an array of feelings and thoughts. To some, the word produces visceral recoil with negative thoughts surfacing of liberalism having a "domino" effect upon the conservatism they desire to hold on to. To others, the word stirs in them a wind of excitement for change; a chance for transformation. Still, to most of us, the word produces confusion at best and arrogance at worst. Postmodernism now invades our culture at various levels and with differing levels of intensity. Some of the shifts invoked by the postmodern wave will prove significant for us, while many others will pass by like mainstream radio hits; for we should remember the words of Qoheleth, "What has been will be again, what has been done will be done again; there is nothing new under the sun" (Ecc. 1:9).

This chapter is the synthesis of my personal desire to see youth ministry transform culture, specifically as I engage Asian American students. I wanted to understand how postmodernism affects students, and understand how to engage it though the lens of Scripture and my commitment to Christ. My goal is not to present the "purpose-driven" Asian American youth ministry, nor is it to provide specific steps on how to do postmodern ministry for Asian Americans. What you should get out of this chapter is a journey through culture and truth resulting in some principles that I have tried addressing in my ministries. We will approach this journey cautiously, excitingly, and in light of our commitment to Christ. This chapter is presented in three sections: the method for synthesis; second, the pertinent aspects of postmodernism; and third, principles that I have applied to my ministries.

While researching youth ministry, one may find a wealth of resources about postmodern youth ministries. However, one will find little to nothing concerning postmodernity in Asian American youth ministry.[1] Therefore, discovering the postmodern impact on Asian youth ministry must happen synthetically: exegeting culture and exegeting faith. One method is researching various sources that specifically address different elements (i.e. postmodern, Christian, Asian American) and merge them to uncover principles. One downfall of this method is the introducing of bias into the study. Since absolute objectivity is not possible, one must at least state their own presuppositions. One may also find that dealing only with theory and opinions of other writers leaves them with significant but superficial conclusions.

Since no writer can ultimately provide the one-size-fits-all model for all ministries, one proven method to synthesis is ethnography. This strategy enables a youth worker to examine both the culture at large and understand its implications based on the culture of their own youth group. Ethnography refers to the qualitative description of human social phenomena, based on fieldwork. Ethnographies allow a youth worker to observe how a body of believers exhibit, practice, and share their faith, providing grounded and realistic observations. Applying ethnographic methods, such as participant observation, interviewing, and mapping (especially of the students' school environments) assist the youth worker in gaining helpful knowledge about the current beliefs and practices of their youth.[2] These methods help to assess cultural impact and minimize the haste of applying postmodern principles without first knowing of its influence upon the group. Furthermore, it is important to observe the culture of your youth at a ground level rather than relying on generalizations made by authors, lest they apply inappropriate, superficial, or even worse, unbiblical principles to the ministry.

To properly address how postmodernism affects Asian American youth ministries, we must discuss the basics of postmodernism.[3] Why should this philosophical term matter to youth ministry? In lieu of a thorough discussion, let us look at two things: 1) its history and development, and 2) its significance. One must note that postmodernism is related to modernism, since postmodernity "involves a rejection of the modern mindset, but launched under the conditions of modernity."[4]

The modern mind began during the Renaissance, which elevated humankind to the center of reality. One particular figure from this time period was Francis Bacon, who had a "vision of humans exercising power over nature by means of the discovery of nature's secrets."[5] Following the Renaissance, the Enlightenment period thrust the individual self to the center of all thought. The prominent figure from this time period was René Descartes, who "laid the philosophical foundation for the modern edifice with his focus on doubt, which led him to conclude that the existence of the thinking self is the first truth that doubt cannot deny."[6] The result of Descartes' work was the definition of human nature as "a thinking substance and the human person as an autonomous rational subject."[7] The scientific framework for modernity was later provided by Isaac Newton, thus solidifying the ideal of modernity which "can appropriately be characterized as Descartes' autonomous, rational substance encountering Newton's mechanistic world."[8] Ultimately, knowledge is seen as being totally accessible to the modern human mind. These assumptions lead one to believe that knowledge is: certain, objective, and good.

The modern mindset was first called into question by Friedrich Nietzsche, but "the full-frontal assault did not begin until the 1970s."[9] This rise of postmodernism came out of deconstruction as a literary theory, which strongly influenced contemporary philosophy. The work of deconstructionists claimed that "meaning is not inherent in a text itself, but emerges only as the interpreter enters into dialogue with the text."[10] They began to abandon the search for an objective and accessible knowledge of reality because they asserted that "the world has no center, only differing viewpoints and perspectives."[11]

Why is this postmodern development important? It is important because it has influenced the mindset of all people. People began to challenge the idea that knowledge is inherently good. Those living in the post-World War II era began to question scientific advancements and their ramifications. Postmodern thought also emphasizes "holism."[12] Knowledge is no longer king because postmodernists assert that the mind is only one part of being a person; there are emotions, intuitions, and more. Not only was there a suspicion of modern ideals, but a rejection of the modern principle of knowledge. To postmodernists, knowledge must be "relative, indeterminate, and participatory."[13]

In other words, no longer is knowledge considered a way to absolute truth because it must be personalized and contextualized. This presents a dilemma for Christians as we want to present Jesus as the absolute truth. Stanley Grenz wisely noted: "It would be ironic—indeed, it would be tragic—if evangelicals ended up as the last defenders of the now dying modernity. To reach people in the new postmodern context, we must set ourselves to the task of deciphering the implications of postmodernism for the gospel."[14]

In order to formulate principles we must also understand Asian Americans. Due to the fact that virtually all published youth ministry resources are directed towards a white, suburban, middle class church, additional work must be done to discern how postmodernism affects Asian youth ministries. Due to limited space, I'll just mention one helpful reference. Paul Tokunaga has penned a chapter entitled "Understanding our Asian DNA,"[15] where he describes traits and qualities that are common among Asian Americans. The five strands of Asian DNA are: "Confucianism, shame, suffering, our families, and liminality." Though this may not apply equally in every context, it is a good starting point to exegete the culture of Asian youth groups.

"Deciphering the implications of postmodernism for the gospel," is our task today, but we should be deciphering culture on a regular basis. A note of caution here: one must tread carefully when adopting any cultural ideas by submitting themselves to the light of Scripture. Without being grounded in the Word, we may be swayed by novelty or experience that is apart from God's revealed will. I must also repeat that these principles are only examples of how I have done things, not guarantees of success especially in light of the volatility of postmodernism and the variety of our individual contexts. Tony Jones says it rightly, "The new paradigm will be up to you. That's because what works in my town probably won't work in yours."[16]

With that said we can move onto my personal discoveries with actively engaging minds. I call for you to be my community of interpretation and to challenge me to sharpen my views and call me out when I am wrong. As with any good ethnographer, one must recognize his own limitations and merits: (1) experience in first generation Chinese churches, (2) mostly affluent suburban areas, (3) my own lack of long-term experience, (4) my own transition from modernity to postmodernity.

One area that postmodernism seems to greatly affect is identity. For Asian-Americans, identity has always been a struggle, and the emergence of postmodernism only heightens the struggle. With postmodernism, "The self is seen as an ever-changing phenomenon that is constantly constructed and reconstructed in and through multiple role performances and constant dialogue with others."[17] This results in a growing and deeper sense of meaninglessness, powerlessness, and hopelessness in the search of identity. But where did modernism fail us in the development of identity? Dean suggests, "For adolescents struggling with identity, sanitizing Christian transition of radicality and transcendence amounted to castration, rendering Christianity impotent for unifying and reordering the self."[18] Adolescents want something to live and "die for" and, in the absence of an absolute truth, are capable of settling for commitments that fall well short of transcendence. In other words, when "Christianity became one more option among literally thousands of others,"[19] teenagers could not find an answer to the deepest questions of identity and significance.

One suggestion to deal with this dilemma is to provide a "larger purposive narrative"[20] that serves as a context in which our individual narratives can find their rightful place. When creating this "larger purposive narrative", one must consider the theme of reconciliation as the key to developing identity. Since Asian Americans deal with such a deep sense of shame that often comes from fathers (or both parents), this rift between parent and child must be addressed.[21] Cha and Jao suggest the parable of the Prodigal Son as one ideal for developing this narrative. One possible result of a loving and compassionate father may "offer them a lasting identity that can provide a sense of purpose, continuity, and hope in this postmodern world."[22]

Another conflict is the Confucian mindset clashing with the postmodern ideals of self. By providing the gospel, Cha and Jao suggest that it will offer "Asian American postmoderns with a core identity that does not change over time, that does not fragment in the multiple, shifting contexts we live in today, and that does not get reduced to a mere collage that lacks coherence."[23]

Ownership of ministry is another way that youth can gain a healthy identity. I have seen this applied through youth leadership teams, where the youth are given leadership over specific ministry needs in the youth group. Such examples include: worship team, greeting team, hospitality team, evangelism team, games team, etc. These opportunities may provide ownership and fostering of identity, but what really makes these responsibilities significant for identity development is when they are supported with discipling. At Wheaton Chinese Alliance Church (WCAC), I have seen their "doulos" (Greek for 'slave') team thrive and develop strong disciples of Christ not just because of the sense of ownership, but also because of the involvement of the youth director and other counselors in the leaders' personal lives. Setting up mentoring relationships (one-on-one's) with students also provides meaningful ways to be sensitive to the identity of the postmodern Asian youth, because it allows students to live life with their mentor. I have seen this take place at camps where students met with adult leaders or mentors during camp to discuss spiritual issues. One thing I have observed regarding mentoring relationships is that placing more than two students in a group seems to weaken the intimacy that is needed to foster meaningful relationships. Also, one must be wary about the match up of student and mentor; the Christian character of the counselor is always the biggest point of concern on my list of qualifications. Outward appearances only provide superficial excitement, while godly character provides a long-term example and solid foundations.

One final principle for fostering individual growth is providing opportunities to share testimonies. At WCAC, we have recently begun testimony times before our bible studies as a way for the group to get to know each other spiritually and to encourage each other. This provides an avenue for the youth to be real about who they are.

While I believe addressing the needs of the individual is a significant start, we also have to address the community as a whole. Identity, in a postmodern setting, ultimately involves the community that the individual is participating in. If modernism brought in a new era of emphasizing the individual, postmodernism is a return to the community (idealistically). Jones describes the community that postmodern youth want to see as "being real" and more relevant; they desire a church that is "a sacred community of persons who follow a mysterious and demanding Lord."[24]

With Asian American youth, we recognize that this "notion of forming self-identity within a community is reinforced by our Confucian-based culture that teaches that our identities are shaped largely by our families."[25] However, not all communities effectively reach out to Asian Americans enough to help them with issues of self-identity; real communities must exert grace, the biblical practice of authority, and also exemplify the Word.[26]

First, a community of grace is one that deals with the shame that is deeply rooted in Asian culture. It may seem overly simplistic to say that grace needs to be shared within an Asian American context, but it often isn't that simple! Cha claims that "many Asian-American young people grow up in immigrant churches where people talk incessantly about their own achievements or of their children."[27] This gossip in turn, shames many students as parents use them to compete with other adults.

The second component of effective community is the biblical practice of power and authority. In Confucian social structure, relationships are rigidly hierarchical; "Our culture sanctions and teaches men's exercise of power over women, parents over children, older versus younger, ruler over ruled, and educated over the less-educated."[28] But postmodernists have cultivated a general suspicion of power and authority. Dean describes this suspicion as a result of the church's adaptation of culture so as to mimic culture's virtual virtuosity.[29] In general, postmodernists look at the family and church as structures which seek to exert power over them, often for the benefit of the institution rather than the individual. How then can we disarm this suspicion? Cha and Jao suggest that we need to "demonstrate that the biblical notion of power and authority is neither abusive nor self-seeking."[30]

Another way to share power is to "grow in the practice of team ministry in the spirit of the priesthood of all believers."[31] Since Asian American churches and youth groups are often run by one person or a group of homogenous people, there needs to be a shift in leadership toward plurality and diversity. One idea suggested to me by a professor is inviting a youth representative on the elder board to be included in the decision-making processes of the church. That surprised me because I've never seen this done before, and it would prove extremely difficult to implement. However, this kind of creative thinking is needed if we want to provide non-threatening leadership in the church.

This type of diversity in leadership can lead to accountability. By removing hierarchy to acknowledge gifts that exist in different parts of the body of Christ, it is possible to truly exemplify how power is laid down for the good of the whole, not the individual. While Asians have an element of this in Confucianism, the element of hierarchy would be removed so that individuals with unique gifts could learn to serve one another and hold each other accountable because of the larger purpose that Christ has redeemed us for. Thus, in order to convey an authentic, yet non-threatening leadership system, the leadership should have "accountability of leaders to one another, to the larger body, and to the head of the church, Jesus our Lord."[32]

Finally, an effective community must be a community of the Word. We are not only to proclaim the Word, but also to exemplify the Word in our lives. This kind of living conveys "a community that interprets the Word faithfully and that 'performs' the Word authentically."[33] One aspect of this is parental involvement. I recognize the large influence of my parents, which is often more significant than anything I ever learned in church or youth group. The community of a youth ministry must actively involve its parents! It is the parents that are the primary teachers of youth (Deut. 6:7). The youth ministry is the bridge that ties all the language ministries within a church because it ministers to all of them by working with their youth. Unfortunately, the youth ministry is often the sole means of spiritual growth for the youth, and lacks the critical element of the parents' involvement. Without this larger adult community involved with the youth, there are irreconcilable gaps in their understanding of the body of Christ. I recognize there are significant cultural and generational gaps that may "seem" to hinder relationships, but we all have one thing in common, Christ. In order to begin involving parents we recommend parent meetings, family meetings, and parent / student panels. One must assess their own parent group before trying any of these, and also get the support of all the pastors so these attempts will be as unifying as possible.

So far, community has been internally-focused, yet community should include the people who surround the church as well. A youth ministry that never knows what is going on with the neighbors of their church (Christian or not) is negligent of the community. At school, students who are involved in project groups are exposed to the reality that is beyond their school. A youth ministry that wants to be sensitive to the communal aspect of postmodernists, must also reach outside its church walls. This can be expressed through missions trips, addressing crises in the community (especially through action!), and being involved in community events (i.e. festivals, concerts, etc.). When I have seen youth groups involved in the community, it is evident that those experiences provide the youth with real-world Christianity experience which allows them to develop their personal identity as a Christian outside of the youth group room.

While returning from a trip to inner city Detroit, I saw that many of my kids were truly blessed by their interaction with inner city kids, and many had a chance to actively share the gospel with them. However, I also learned that there is a strong danger of becoming "me-focused" even during outreach-focused events. I first saw this in the testimonies given by some of the students from the event; they focused on how they impacted the kids and what they learned. They still lacked a grasp of how God was involved and how He was working in and through them. We need to provide opportunities for community involvement, but they should never be the same as a service group at the local high school. Emphasis should be placed on the fact that the desire to serve the community comes as our understanding of God's love for people and how He desires to work through us.

Finally, I will mention the "silent exodus," and how community can be a medium to help remedy this growing issue.[34] In a discussion with my youth ministry group at Trinity about this issue of the "silent exodus" (this problem exists in all churches, not just Asian ones), our discussion led to the subject of the lack of connection between church youth leaders and the leaders of parachurch organizations. I realize that church leaders may have differing thoughts regarding parachurches, but I believe a partnership may be a way to provide a smooth transition for our youth into and out of college. One way we can do this is to actively communicate with parachurch leaders of the colleges our youth are going to and connect our youth with them before they arrive on campus. On the other hand, parachurches should connect their students with church pastors of the cities they are moving to. We are missing out on powerful possibilities for ministry and growth without a partnership through this transition. Nearly all of our youth go to secular colleges, and if we assume they will find a church / fellowship group on their own, we run a great risk of them leaving the church for good. During the senior year of youth group, I see it as absolutely essential to provide intellectual and practical preparation for our students. This can happen by providing resources and specific lessons to teach our students how to engage in intellectual debates, as well as how to continue to grow spiritually during college. The parachurch should not be seen as a threat to our churches, but as a wonderful continuation for our own youth ministries. By teaming up, we can put an end to the "silent exodus".

During my ethnography and research, I also found a growing desire for transcendence in today's youth. Between the 1960s and the 1990s, "Protestant worship became vacuous and had lost its ability to relate to the people in the pews."[35] This gave rise to what Jones calls the "Tyranny of Immanence," where "The closeness of Jesus to the individual believer has been emphasized at the expense of the majesty of God."[36] What is the answer? Jones claims that a shift toward transcendence is needed. In his definition, transcendence acknowledges that much of God's universe is irreconcilable, irresolvable, contradictory, and mysterious.[37] Dean claims that we need a shift to transcendence because "only a transcendent ideology is worthy of an investment of self."[38] She also claims that transcendence has the ability to move people. This is based on the claim that "the single most important criterion for excellence during adolescence is, 'Did it move me?'"[39] The overemphasis of immanence is a valid critique upon current youth ministry practices; however, I don't think moving to this other extreme of transcendence is going to further our goals either.

There needs to be a balance of such ideas. Transcendence and immanence are both important because our God is both wholly other and yet intimately involved in His creation. This becomes evermore important because our youth come from a Confucian understanding of education that elevates immanence. Generally, they tend to see good grades as the way to a good life; because grades are the means to good colleges, which in turn lead to good jobs, to then provide financial stability to their families. The focus is on the here and now, which conveys that the world has priority. If we reinforce the idea that Christianity is only about here and now, they miss the majesty of God and his larger purpose for our lives.

We can begin addressing the need to balance transcendence and immanence in the way we worship. In our prayers, do we have a theology that subconsciously sees God as some vending machine that provides a desired product with the correct amount of prayer or the right words? Prayer must not be like some laundry list; it must include our acknowledgment and reverence of our God, what He has made, what He has done in the past, and His promises to act now and in the future. Regarding praise, are the songs really about a worthy and holy God? Or have much of the worship songs led in our youth groups been relegated to self-focus and self-need? It is great to sing about how much you love the Lord, but that means nothing without recognition of who God is and what He has done!

Seeing the balance of immanence and transcendence of God has impacted our students' spiritual lives significantly. One of our students' father had been in and out of cancer treatment for some time. While on a mission trip, the student received a call with the news that his Dad was again diagnosed with cancer. I know he felt sadness and a bit of helplessness being away from his family, so I asked him how he dealt with it. His response was a genuine peace that God had a plan and that he knew God was in control. I do not know if our theology or worship directly impacted that response or not, but I know that if our focus was narcissistic, instead of theocentric, that kind of response would not even be fathomable.

Experience and participation is another component that is essential for our postmodern Asian youth. One key idea is to redirect their suspicion of the church towards truth in happenings. Dean provides us a good explanation, "Postmodern youth invest their fidelity in happenings ("Hey, what's happening?"), not in static confessions of faith. Institutions do not "happen"; they are.[40]

This leads to another element, participation. Participation is the means by which postmodernists make their faith personal and relative: "Postmodern youth view truth as highly personal, both in the sense that they want experience it personally, and in the sense that truth is most provocatively encountered in the form of a person who is true to them."[41] It is here that we can see Cha and Jao's "Community of the Word" taking place. This is essential to our youth because they have been placed in systems of hierarchal structure their entire lives, often being abandoned by them.[42] They need ways to express their faith, not just know about their faith. Youth do not learn solely by lecture, they learn by being involved. I find myself asking, "Why are schools aware of the variety of learning styles, but the church is not?"

As suggested before, youth leadership teams and discipleship are ways to provide interactive experiences. Experience and participation should also shape how we teach. Being in junior high ministry, I may have 10-20 minutes of their attention before they find something better to amuse themselves with (one student constructed an entire battle scene with paper cups and paper clips; I was quite amused). However, if my teaching involves something they can touch, hear, smell, or see, their attention and capacity to learn increases. I used to teach a lesson on praise psalms by describing what they were and showing examples of them in Scripture. However, I realized that they held onto the concept of praise a lot fuller if they were allowed to bring in CDs of music, instruments to play, and share poems that they have written. This participation for them to interact with the idea of praise, and discuss amongst themselves what praise was and what praise was not.

Regarding sermons, I have recently rediscovered a love for narrative and story. Most of us think the quintessential message is a Pauline epistle that is preached with a proposition that leads to three points. However, our youth's lives are stories, their whole world of TV and entertainment is story-based. I have tried incorporating narrative sermons and narrative introductions in my Sunday school lessons. Sermons are developed more inductively rather than deductively. The benefit to that is holding off the proposition till the end. Youth like to be held in suspense; who would want to read Harry Potter if they knew what was going to happen already? They seem to respond to the sermons and remember more than the didactic style in which I was taught in Bible college and seminary. This does not mean that exegesis and study of the biblical passage is neglected. To the contrary, I find developing narrative sermons to be much more difficult as it is built upon the same study, but requires more creative forms of delivery.

As for Sunday school lessons, beginning with a story sets the tone for the class. During a Sunday school class, it is done in an inductive/deductive style. I often introduce the lesson with a story (either made up, or researched from somewhere) which leads to a principle or general direction for the lesson. Then revisit the points again during the rest of the class, expanding on specific points of interest. The experience of a narrative seems to draw their attention deeper than explaining deductive principles.

Finally, postmodernists are crying out for authenticity. This is one theme that runs throughout postmodern literature. The structures in society failed them because they proposed to be truth without displaying it; they claimed belief but didn't live it. I left this one for last because I believe this is the most important attitude to demonstrate in our ministries. A shift towards authenticity requires that the church be different than the world. Jones points out the problem of imitating the world and the action to counter what I call "hyper-relevance":

When we water down the message of Christ, or when we try to market the church so that it looks like a shopping mall or a university or a counseling center—or when we pretend that we're no different than a hundred other organizations—we're not being church. *The church is different. And to be taken seriously, we must be on guard, always measuring our youth ministries in terms of their authenticity and integrity.*[43] [*Italics* mine]

How do we be authentic in our ministries? First, our teaching and preaching must be lived out. We must run weekly check-ups to see if what we are teaching is consistent with how it is lived out daily. We should be transparent, but never for the sake of just becoming friends with our youth. Authenticity is important, but it doesn't mean that our righteousness before God is compromised. Second, our ministries must always reflect our motivation and purpose. It is important to perform regular evaluations about the group and the youth pastor, and also the students, parents, and other staff in the church. Without this form of accountability, programs may become unbiblical at worst and unaware of our students at best.

The five principles I have discussed are not exhaustive, nor will they prove to be effective for every ministry. I have explained my method of developing principles, but I must also disclose my convictions and my theology of youth ministry. First, I acknowledge academic writings on this issue, but never forsake the gospel. As youth workers, I believe it is important to be informed about secular culture, academia, and what fellow believers are saying about culture, but it doesn't require us to force the gospel into "new" worldviews and cultural ideals. The gospel transcends culture and time. This means that Scripture informs how I think and how I view the rest of the world, not the other way around.

Second, I have a commitment to the unity of the Body of Christ. Though I support diversity within the unity of the body of Christ, what I am opposed to is the misconception that postmodernists must distance themselves from their "modern" forefathers to accomplish their own goals. We should remember that our unity is something Jesus prayed for and that it will testify to the rest of the world of who Christ is (John 17:20-26). In our bi-cultural churches, this means that we don't reject our first generational roots simply for their lack of postmodern adherence. This also means that parents are always welcome and cared for to the best of our ability. I believe that God's purpose of the family to be a primary place of spiritual education should not be replaced nor undermined by our youth ministries.

In researching postmodernism and youth ministry, I've read numerous books and articles. One conclusion I can confidently state is that postmodernism is understood differently by everyone! But we are not left with a nihilistic end; no, we have confidence in our Lord Jesus Christ. Wading through postmodernism may seem overwhelming, but we will find that its challenges sharpen us and its merits will uplift us. Commit yourself to be a student of culture, a lover of students, a learner of Scripture, and a worshiper of God. It is by the grace of God that we are given this honorable task of working with youth, and it will always be God that sustains us. Remember, postmodernism isn't something new to God, and shouldn't be something terrifying to us because nothing is new under the sun.

NOTES

[1] One may find articles addressing the issue of the "Silent Exodus," but not specifically with youth ministry in an Asian setting. The term "Silent Exodus" was notably introduced by the article cited in note #34 below.

[2] Two resources on ethnography: David M. Fetterman, *Ethnography: Step by Step* (Newbury Park, CA: Sage Publications, 1989), and Margaret D. LeCompte and Jean J. Schensul, *Designing & Conducting Ethnographic Research* (Walnut Creek, CA: AltaMira Press, 1999).

[3] To be more informed about postmodernism, please refer to the bibliography.

[4] Stanley Grenz, *A Primer on Postmodernism* (Grand Rapids: Eerdmans, 1996), 2.

[5] Ibid.

[6] Ibid., 3.

[7] Ibid.

[8] Ibid.

[9] Ibid., 5.

[10] Ibid., 6.

[11] Ibid., 7.

[12] Ibid.

[13] Ibid.

[14] Ibid., 10.

[15] Paul Tokunaga, *Invitation to Lead* (Downers Grove, IL: InterVarsity Press, 2003), 32-51.

[16] Tony Jones, *Postmodern Youth Ministry* (Grand Rapids: Zondervan, 2001), 12.

[17] Peter Cha and Greg Jao, "Reaching Out to Postmodern Asian-Americans" in *Telling the Truth*, ed. D.A. Carson (Grand Rapids: Zondervan, 2000), 228.

[18] Krenda Creasy Dean, "X-Files and Unknown Gods: The Search for Truth with Postmodern Adolescents," *American Baptist Quarterly* 19, no. 1 (2000): 8.

[19] Ibid.

[20] Cha and Jao, 229.

[21] Recently I was speaking with a fellow youth worker and recognized that about 80% of our youth grow up in highly dysfunctional families, thus adding to the importance of reconciliation.

[22] Cha and Jao, 231.

[23] Ibid.

[24] Jones, *Postmodern Youth Ministry*, 90.

[25] Cha and Jao, 232.

[26] Ibid., 233.

[27] Ibid., 235.

[28] Ibid.

[29] Dean, "X-Files and Unknown Gods," 11.

[30] Cha and Jao, 235.

[31] Ibid.

[32] Ibid., 237.

[33] Ibid.

34 Helen Lee, "Silent Exodus : Can the East Asian church in America reverse the flight of its next generation?" *Christianity Today* 40 (1996), 50-53. I have furthered developed ideas on how to foster genuine growth out of community/missions projects. The biggest challenge is that the positive potential of short-term projects is not automatic— ethnocentrism and materialism still exists; commitment to giving is not automatic. The most common response to missions trips is their change to be more "grateful," or "thankful." These are good changes, but that is missing the connection to the local community. Also, interethnic relationships are largely unchanged as well. There is a stigma to overseas or distance trips that is almost lofty and honorable. They now can put "service project" on their college applications. But is there any real change to helping those in need around their homes/churches? We need to be more conscious of linking the local to the global. We can do this by building into training time to spend in other contexts and to interview/visit with a person from another culture.

35 Jones, 95.

36 Ibid.

37 Ibid., 97.

38 Dean, 14.

39 Ibid.

40 Dean, 12.

41 Ibid.

42 Chap Clark, *Hurt: Inside the World of Today's Teenagers* (Grand Rapids, MI: Baker, 2004). This is probably the best book on youth I have read. His ethnographic study is well done and insightful.

43 Jones, 90.

12

The Humility and Reality of Ministry

Joseph Tsang

At the conclusion of the Youthworkers Forum, we heard these clos-
ing words as a commission and challenge for how the call to Asian
American youth ministry is a call to humility. I found these
thoughts to be sobering, honest, and helpful. It provides perspec-
tive beyond the techniques, plans, and studies. May this edited
transcript offer wisdom for your calling to the people and place
you'd serve to the glory of God.

Before we look at what the apostle Paul is calling us to do in Philippians 2:1-11 as ministers, I wanted to share a few random thoughts
on postmodernism that was briefly discussed during the Forum. Since
technically I'm no longer in youth ministry and have moved onto adult
ministry, I didn't want to get in the way of the conversation going on,
so that people in the trenches could get the answers they needed rather
than having my own intellectual curiosities satiated.

From my sense of things, the next thing after postmodernism is on
its way. New theories are being discussed. During a visit to the University of Chicago, I saw a sign posted saying postmodernism is dead. I
asked when that sign had been put up and the response was 1995; a
ways back. If modernity is the belief that given enough time and resources, we will find the truth and it will be objective; if postmodernity
is the belief that there is no truth with a "capital T" and that all truth is
merely subjective, hence truth is only true for you; then truth comes
from the same place: ultimately us! We are the source of truth, according to modernism and postmodernism. I believe the next wave of
thinking will be a neo-classicalism, where we affirm that the truth is not
in us. The truth comes from a source outside of us. This is great because it is consistent with what we believe about revelation. This line of
thinking will assert that truth is outside of ourselves and relational,
namely found in relationship with Jesus Christ.

Now, let's take a closer look at our passage, Philippians 2:1-11. This was written as an exhortation to all followers of Christ, but it can also speak specifically to us as ministers to be humble. For example, hip-hop is here to stay and dominates our youth culture. Guitar-driven music is less and less of an influence. In a few years, the guitar may look to kids like the accordion looks to us! I say this as a call to humility. We need to have humility in the way we approach our worship music styles. We may be on the way out in our musical tastes. We can only reach out to who we can reach. The people we're called to and the people we can actually reach are a small niche—that should be another reason for humility. Be yourselves and reach those you're called to.

Let's think a bit more about what humility means. What is Paul calling us to do in humility? In churches everywhere, it's almost epidemic and yet normal for ministers to quit and leave their ministries. From the stories I have heard, it seems that the average stay is three years or less. In the Asian church, one of the main reasons is because it is painful to work in the church.

This Youthworkers Forum almost got there for me. But we didn't quite get there and say what needed to be said. We need to acknowledge that the church is composed of sinful people who sometimes go unchecked. If our churches are so great, why do ministers pack it up so quickly? Our actions betray what we really believe. For example, at liberal seminaries, often they teach the intrinsic goodness of people; humans are basically good folks! But then why do they spend such enormous funds on sophisticated security systems for their theological libraries armed with lasers, metal vault-like doors and gates? Contrast this with Wheaton College, where I attended, which teaches the depravity of man but has such a lax security system in their library that makes it easy to walk out with anything you would like. Our actions betray what we believe. And what does it say about our churches when so many ministers leave?

I cannot address it from the churches' side but I can address it from the minister's side. The reason we leave ministry is because we have the wrong dreams.

I forget who told this story. It was either Craig Barnes, Henri Nouwen, or Eugene Peterson. I think maybe it was Craig Barnes' graduation when Henri Nouwen came to speak. I read these guys so much, they're all a blur. But at a seminary graduation, a speaker rallied the recent grads into a frenzy. He asked, "Do you love my sheep?"

"Yes!" they cheered.

Again, "Do you love my sheep?"

"Yes!" they escalated.

Of course, one more time, "Do you love my sheep?"

"Yes!" they roared a final time.

Prepared for a call to feed the sheep, the audience instead received this warning, "Then be prepared to go to meetings—endless meetings. And be prepared to have the same conversations—the same boring conversations over and over. Be prepared to answer the same questions again and again."

And if you are in youth ministry, I would add, be prepared to play the same games! Plan the same meetings! Do the same activities! Answer the same questions! Long-term youth ministry is the discipline of doing the same things over and over, year after year with different teens, because the maturity of the group never changes. It's the same age range every year. So be prepared to give the same talks about dating, parents, other religions, and being asked how far is too far. Also, be prepared to be underappreciated, maybe even underpaid. Be prepared to be criticized. In short, be prepared to be used. When we first prayed: "Lord, use me!" —why are we later surprised when we feel used? Not that we are only to be exploited by God in ministry. We do encounter tremendous blessings; we do have incredible experiences including deep communion with God during the course of ministry.

The issue with having the wrong dreams for our ministries is this: what we all seek is resurrection, but we forget that there is only one way to get there. Most pastors leave after a few years, two to three; but ironically, polls show that the best years of ministry are usually years four to fifteen. Within three years, it seems and feels like the church wants to kill us. Does that sound familiar? The first year, they're open to hearing your message. The second year, they're still checking you out. Then by the third year, they don't like where you're leading the people so they decide to get rid of you. They may even crucify you. But we won't let them.

This is what I learned accidentally as I stayed at my church for eleven years. I didn't want to be a part of the same story line of ministers not getting along: "I hate you"; "You hate me"; "We can't get along"; so, we split! I "accidentally" laid my life down on the cross for them. I say "accidentally" because I thought of leaving every day! The way I stayed was to ask myself if I could do one more day. Yes, one more day. Woody Allen said that 90% of life is just showing up. And I continued to show up until I gave my life to my church—willing to be used; willing to suffer; willing to give up my rights; willing to take on the wounds of Jesus; willing to die to self; and in that daily willingness, finding resurrection.

I think Paul is calling us in Philippians to lay down our lives for our churches—to stay and follow Jesus to the cross. In your twenties as a minister, I would advise aiming to stay at your church for five years. That would be a good run.

The need to move is built into us. Junior high was three years. High school was four years. College was four years or maybe seven for some of us. So during our first job, around year three, we get itchy. And if we see the church building that cross and buying nails, we're out of there! We move around because we hate the feeling of being left behind. No one wants to be left behind (there's a whole series of books about that!). I would advise not jumping without a place to land. In other words, don't leave or jump ship unless there is a definitive place to land. In my mind, that's another church or another place calling you. And if you leave, do your best to leave well instead of burning bridges. A good sign you left well is if you have the ability to return to your former place of employment with minimal or no awkwardness.

In your thirties, I would advise trying to stay for ten years. In our thirties, too many variables are still in flux. But in as much as you can control, learn faithfulness to your church. And in your forties, I hope you can find the church that you will give your life to. If you are still church-hopping, especially as a minister in your forties and fifties, you probably need to re-evaluate your understanding of the call of the cross.

Tell Jesus stories. Go to the cross for each other. Forgive each other. If we cannot forgive each other, we have no message. If we cannot forgive each other, we have no hope. If two brothers or sisters who claim to know God, cannot work something out and be reconciled, what chance does a world that does not know God have? Our message is about amazing grace and reconciliation.

I close with a remix of a song[1] that your teens probably listen to, as a challenge:

Welcome to the planet / Welcome to existence

Everyone's here / Everyone's here

Everybody's watching you now / Everybody waits for you now

What happens next? / What happens next?

Welcome to the fallout / Welcome to resistance

The tension is here / The tension is here

Between who you are and who you could be / Between how it is and how it should be.

Maybe redemption has stories to tell / Maybe forgiveness is right where you fell

Where can you run to escape from yourself? / Where you gonna go?

Where you gonna go? / Salvation is here.

I dare you to *stay* / I dare you to *stay*

I dare you to let *God* lift *you* off the floor

I dare you to *stay* / I dare you to *stay*

Like today never happened / Today never happened

Today never happened / Today never happened before.

NOTES

[1] Remix based on lyrics from the song by Switchfoot titled "I Dare You to Move" from the album "Learning to Breathe" on the Chordant label, 2000.

Postscript

Paul & Alice Chou
Co-Founders of L² Foundation

God has a unique calling for everyone. From the experience of raising our own three children especially during the challenging adolescent years, we find it most critical to help teens lay a strong biblical foundation as they begin to discover their identities, mold their worldviews and pursue the understanding of God's calling. We need to raise up strong, healthy, progressive leaders for our next generation.

Asian American youth are uniquely positioned by God to grow up in a bi-cultural world. They learn from the traditional Asian heritage of their immigrant parents where hard work, discipline, respect and humility are highly valued. Plus, they are educated in an American environment that encourages self-expression, creativity and leadership. Benefiting from both worlds, they can make a great impact for God's Kingdom as they seek to live as disciples of Jesus Christ and respond to God's calling.

We proudly affirm the work of the many youth workers who have invested their time and energy into our Asian American youth. We realize your work is often challenging, seemingly unfruitful and falling on deaf ears. We want to assure you those ears are not deaf, and God himself is responsible for His own. His words and your labor of love will not return void. We are grateful for the many contributors who have made this book a valuable resource. We hope this conversation will continue, and together we can and will build up the next generation of leaders that will be a blessing to the world.

Bibliography

ASIAN AMERICAN

Carnes, Tony and Fenggang Yang. *Asian American Religions: The Making and Remaking of Borders and Boundaries.* New York: New York University Press, 2004.

Cha, Peter and Greg Jao. "Reaching Out to Postmodern Asian-Americans." *Telling the Truth.* Edited by D.A. Carson. Grand Rapids: Zondervan, 2000.

Cha, Peter, S. Steve Kang, and Helen Lee. *Growing Healthy Asian American Churches.* Downers Grove, IL: InterVarsity Press, 2006.

Chang, Curtis . "Second-Generation Ministry at the Boston Chinese Evangelical Church." 1993. <http://www.egc.org/research/Issue_2/>

Chong, Kelly. "What It Means To Be Christian: The Role of Religion in the Construction of Ethnic Identity and Boundary Among Second-Generation Korean Americans." *Sociology of Religion.* 58 (1998).

Ebaugh, Helen Rose and Janet Saltzman Chafetz. *Religion and the New Immigrants: Continuities and Adaptations in Immigrant Congregations.* New York: AltaMira Press, 2000.

Fong, Ken U. *Pursuing the Pearl: A Comprehensive Resource for Multi-Asian Ministry.* Valley Forge, PA: Judson Press, 1999.

Gelder, Craig Van. *Confident Witness—Changing World: Rediscovering the Gospel in North America.* Grand Rapids: Eerdmans, 1999.

Jeung, Russell. *Faithful Generations: Race and New Asian American Churches.* New Brunswick, NJ: Rutgers University Press, 2005.

Kitano, Harry H. L. and Roger Daniels. *Asian Americans: Emerging Minorities.* New Jersey: Prentice Hall, 1995.

Latourette, Kenneth Scott. *The Chinese: Their History and Culture.* New York: MacMillan Publishing, 1964.

Lee, Helen. "Silent Exodus : Can the East Asian church in America reverse the flight of its next generation?" *Christianity Today* 40 (1996) : 50-53.

Lee, Stacey J. *Unraveling the "Model Minority" Stereotype: Listening to Asian American Youth.* New York: Teachers College Press, 1996.

Ling, Samuel, and Clarence Cheuk. *The "Chinese" Way of Doing Things: Perspectives on America-Born Chinese and the Chinese Church in North America.* San Gabriel: China Horizon, and Vancouver, B.C.: Horizon Ministries Canada, 1999.

Matsuoka, Fumitaka. *Out of Silence: Emerging Themes in Asian American Churches.* Cleveland, OH: United Church Press, 1995.

Min, Pyong Gap. *Asian Americans: Contemporary Trends and Issues.* Thousand Oaks: Sage Publications, 1995.

Moore, Charles A., ed. *The Chinese Mind: Essentials of Chinese Philosophy and Culture.* Honolulu: University of Hawaii Press, 1967.

Ng, David. *People on the way: Asian North Americans discovering Christ, culture, and community.* Valley Forge, PA: Judson Press, 1996.

Rah, Soong-Chan. "The Story of the English-Speaking Asian-American Ministries in Greater Boston." April, 2004.
<http://www.egc.org/research/Issue_2/>

Tokunaga, Paul. *Invitation to Lead: Guidance for Emerging Asian American Leaders.* Downers Grove, IL: InterVarsity Press, 2003.

Quon, Victor. "Teenagers in the Chinese Church," in *Challenger*, Chinese Christian Mission USA, Feb-Mar 2001. Also available at
http://www.l2foundation.org/news/newsID.29/news_detail.asp

Yang, Fenggang. *Chinese Christians in America: conversion, assimilation, and adhesive identities.* University Park, PA: Pennsylvania State University Press, 1999.

Yep, Jeanette, et al. *Following Jesus Without Dishonoring Your Parents.* Downers Grove, IL: InterVarsity Press, 1998.

POSTMODERNISM

Dean, Krenda Creasy, ed. *Growing up Postmodern.* Princeton, NJ: Institute for Youth Ministry, 1998.

Dean, Krenda Creasy. "X-Files and Unknown Gods: The Search for Truth with Postmodern Adolescents." *American Baptist Quarterly* 19 (2000) no. 1 : 3-21.

Flory, Richard W. and Donald E. Miller. *Gen X Religion.* New York, Routlege, 2000.

Grenz, Stanley. *A Primer on Postmodernism.* Grand Rapids: Eerdmans, 1996.

Jones, Tony. *Postmodern Youth Ministry.* Grand Rapids: Zondervan, 2001.

Neufield, Tim. "Postmodern Models of Youth Ministry." *Direction* 31 (2002) no. 2 : 194-205.

SOCIAL JUSTICE

Gutman, Roy and D. Rieff, ed. *Crimes of War: What the Public Should Know.* New York: W.W. Norton, 1999.

Haugen, Gary. *Good News About Injustice: A Witness of Courage in a Hurting World.* Downers Grove, IL: Intervarsity Press, 1999.

Haugen, Gary. *Good News About Injustice: Youth Edition.* Downers Grove, IL: Intervarsity Press, 1999.

Ishay, Micheline R., ed. *The Human Rights Reader: Major Political Writings, Essays, Speeches, and Documents from the Bible to Present.* New York: Routledge, 1997.

Stott, John. *Issues Facing Christians Today.* London: HarperCollins Religious, 1980.

YOUTH & FAMILY MINISTRY

Balswick, Jack O., and Judith K. Balswick. *The Family: A Christian Perspective on the Contemporary Home,* 2nd ed. Grand Rapids, MI: Baker Books, 1999.

Clark, Chap. *Hurt: Inside the World of Today's Teenagers.* Grand Rapids, MI: Baker, 2004.

Clark, Chap et al. *Starting Right.* Grand Rapids, MI: Zondervan, 2001.

Dean, Kenda Creasy, and Ron Foster. *The Godbearing Life: The Art of Soul Tending for Youth Ministry.* Nashville, TN: Upper Room Books, 1998.

Dean, Kenda Creasy. *Practicing Passion: Youth and the Quest for a Passionate Church.* Grand Rapids, MI: Eerdmans, 2004.

DeVries, Mark. *Family-Based Youth Ministry.* Downers Grove, IL: InterVarsity Press, 1994.

Fields, Doug. *Purpose-Driven® Youth Ministry: 9 Essential Foundations for Healthy Growth.* Grand Rapids: Zondervan, 1998.

Group Magazine <http://www.groupmag.com>.

Johnston, Ray. *Developing Student Leaders.* El Cajon, CA: Youth Specialties, 1992.

National Network of Youth Ministries. <http://www.youthworker.net>.

Youth Specialties <http://www.youthspecialties.com>.

About the Contributors

Joey Chen is a seminary student that is devoted to loving and equipping students, and continues to deepen his ministry by engaging church and education. He ministers at Wheaton Chinese Alliance Church, in Wheaton, IL. While ministering in bi-cultural churches he views youth ministry as a means to cultivate unity in the church and an avenue to transform culture.

Brian Gomes is an Associate Pastor overseeing the English ministry and leads the Junior High, High School and College ministries at Chinese Faith Baptist Church in Portland, Oregon. He holds a B.A. in Speech Communication from Western Washington University and a M.Div. from Multnomah Biblical Seminary. He has been serving faithfully in the Chinese community of Portland, Oregon, for 5+ years.

Brian Hall is the founder and area director of Asian Young Life in New Jersey, making a difference among Asian American teenagers, especially the unchurched. He also works as a high school social studies teacher. He holds a Ph.D. in sociology from Rutgers University, where he studied the growth of Christian religion among Chinese American college students. Website: <http://asian.younglife.org>

Eugene Kim currently serves as Minister of Youth and Missions at Chinese Baptist Church of Orange County in Anaheim, California. He has served in this position since 1999. He is a graduate of University of California Irvine and Talbot Seminary. He was instrumental in starting up the RYCE ministry (Retreat for Young Chinese Evangelicals), a ministry serving over a dozen Chinese Baptist churches in Southern California.

Danny Kwon has been serving 14 years in youth ministry, 11 years leading the youth ministry at Yuong Sang Church outside Philadelphia. He teaches Youth Ministry at Covenant Seminary and has written numerous articles for various publications. He holds degrees from Westminster and Covenant Seminary. Along with his love for sports, eating, and making people laugh, he speaks frequently at both youth and youth worker events nationally and internationally.

Caleb Lai currently serves as one of the youth interns for Austin Chinese Church in Austin, Texas. He was born and raised as a pastor's kid, and graduated from the University of Texas at Austin. He came to a realization that middle school and high school students were incredibly excited about God's heart if they were led in the right direction. These years are some of the most important years in any person's life and that God will use young people to change our culture.

Angela Lee is the Youth Director at Evangelical Chinese Bible Church in Vancouver, British Columbia, Canada. She oversees the High School Fellowship, Youth Lighthouse. Her guiding principle for youth ministry: "God looks at the heart" (1 Samuel 16:7). This guiding principle sets the tone for what she seeks to achieve in youth ministry.

Victor Quon is the Youth & College Pastor at River of Life Christian Church in Santa Clara, CA and is the Director of The Malachi 4.6 Network. He has spent 20 years in youth ministry with four different churches in California. The Holy Spirit has taken Victor on a path that led him to developing a multicultural youth ministry in an immigrant Chinese church. Website: <http://www.m46.org>

Cheryl Seid is a 5th generation, Chinese American, native to San Francisco, CA. She attends the Salvation Army—Asian American Corps and was a participant in the Chinese Christian Union basketball league for many years. She currently works for Young Life in the SF Golden Gate area primarily serving Asian American youth.

Joseph Tsang grew up in the small town of New York City. He's a graduate of Wheaton College. He has been a youth pastor for over ten years, most recently at the Chinese Bible Church of Maryland. He recently started serving as Pastor of Vision Church in New York City. Joseph travels for fun, enjoys reading, and is a huge U2 fan. He has been married to Theresa Pak since 2003, also a U2 fan.

Peter Wang has worked with youth since 1995, and developed a youth ministry from 30 to 180 students. He currently serves as the English pastor for a new church plant focused on young Asian Americans, and is creating a non-profit organization (OverFlow Ministries) dedicated to developing Asian American Christian leadership. Peter's approach to youth ministry draws on his cross-cultural experiences as an adolescent immigrant from Taiwan.

Justin Young is the Youth Director at the Chinese Community Church of Indianapolis. Since 1999, he has enjoyed the unique challenges and blessings ministering in a city with a small, but growing, Asian population brings. He hopes his experiences will help other Asian churches in similar contexts.

About L² Foundation

L² Foundation ("L-Squared") is a private foundation that seeks to develop the leadership and legacy of Asian Americans by providing support and resources. L² serves ministry and professional leaders, empowering them to fulfill God's calling.

Founded by Paul & Alice Chou in September 2000, L² Foundation was launched in response to the paucity and struggles of Asian Americans serving as leaders in the society at large. While growing numbers of Asian Americans have succeeded professionally, L² sees a need to channel that success towards strategic sharing of resources and experience to the next generations.

L² Foundation has been engaging in dialogue with innovative and progressive Asian American leaders to explore strategic solutions for developing enduring programs and resources for long-term impact.

L² Foundation does this by hosting occasional gatherings with key leaders from around the nation. L² Foundation has also compiled a free web-based resource center with links, books, articles, and other resources of interest to Asian American leaders and legacy makers. At the time of this writing, there are over 350 resources listed.

L² Foundation looks forward to hearing from you and exploring how we can together serve the Kingdom of God. We'd love to hear from leaders who are actively developing others to their full potential. We also hope to walk alongside of like-minded people who are leaving a legacy of empowering the next generations of Asian Americans, so that they can fulfill God's calling on their lives to make an impact in the world.

L² Foundation
P.O. Box 42126
Washington, DC 20015

Email: office@L2Foundation.org

Web: http://www.L2Foundation.org